A Guide to Crisis Intervention

Kristi Kanel

CENGAGE
Learning™

Australia • Brazil • Japan • Korea • Mexico • Singapore • Spain • United Kingdom • United States

CENGAGE
Learning™

A Guide to Crisis Intervention

Kristi Kanel

Executive Editor:
 Maureen Staudt
 Michael Stranz

Senior Project Development Manager:
 Linda de Stefano

Marketing Specialist:
 Sara Mecurio
 Lindsay Shapiro

Production/Manufacturing Manager:
 Donna M. Brown

PreMedia Supervisor:
 Joel Brennecke

Rights & Permissions Specialist:
 Kalina Hintz
 Todd Osborne

Cover Image:
 Getty Images*

Source: A Guide to Crisis Intervention, 3e, Kristi Kanel, 0495077765, 2007 Brooks Cole

ISBN-13: 978-1-111-06742-7

ISBN-10: 1-111-06742-2

Cengage Learning
5191 Natorp Boulevard
Mason, Ohio 45040
USA

Cengage Learning is a leading provider of customized learning solutions with office locations around the globe, including Singapore, the United Kingdom, Australia, Mexico, Brazil, and Japan. Locate your local office at: **international.cengage.com/region**

Cengage Learning products are represented in Canada by Nelson Education, Ltd.

For your lifelong learning solutions, visit **www.cengage.com/custom**

Visit our corporate website at **www.cengage.com**

Printed in the United States of America
1 2 3 4 5 6 7 12 11 10 09 08

ETHICAL AND PROFESSIONAL ISSUES

CHAPTER 3

THE NEED FOR ETHICS

Strong ethical practice is especially important in the field of crisis intervention because clients in crisis come to a counselor in a vulnerable state of disequilibrium and instability. To take advantage of someone in such an unsteady state would be easy. At the outset of counseling, clients often feel hopeless and scared. They may view a counselor who reaches out with empathy with seemingly all the answers as a hero or savior of some type. Crisis interventionists must adhere to strong ethical behaviors to help clients see them and their abilities in a realistic light.

USE OF PARAPROFESSIONALS

Some mental health professionals may feel that crisis intervention should be provided only by professionals, counselors with at least a masters degree or a license. However, as discussed in Chapter 2, crisis intervention began with the use of community workers, sometimes referred to as nonprofessionals or paraprofessionals. These workers often functioned in multidisciplinary team settings such as county agencies and grassroots nonprofit organizations. Effective crisis intervention can be conducted by undergraduate student trainees or community volunteers as well as by graduate-level students and professional counselors if their training is appropriate and they are properly supervised.

The use of the paraprofessional crisis worker has continued to be especially important as the world has moved into the 21st century. The economic recession of the early 1990s plus a decided shift in governmental policies during the beginning of the 21st century has led to cutbacks in government spending on human services programs, which has meant less money or no money to pay mental health workers. Under these circumstances, the use of volunteers and paraprofessionals makes excellent economic sense, because most professional therapists will not provide crisis intervention consistently for the lowered fees often paid to many paraprofessionals. Also, many situations—including the AIDS epidemic, terrorism, and family deterioration—ensure that crises will be plentiful and intervention desired. When immediate low-cost help is needed, using paraprofessionals makes the community stronger by ensuring that its population is functioning and coping with stress.

SELF-AWARENESS AND COUNTERTRANSFERENCE

Self-awareness is available to crisis workers if they are willing to bring themselves into the interview therapeutically. **Therapeutic awareness** means being conscious of one's own emotions, values, opinions, and behavior. Understanding one's own psychological processes and dynamics can help one guide others through their processes (Corey, Corey, & Callanan, 1993, pp. 30–32). Students can learn therapeutic awareness in crisis intervention classes; such training can help students take an honest, in-depth look at themselves in relation to the crisis of interest. It can be a valuable learning experience, enhancing the crisis worker's skills in helping clients. If workers learn to deal with all the issues surrounding AIDS, for example, they have a better chance of helping a client deal with them.

Countertransference, an issue that must often be addressed in the helping professions, is defined as an "unconsciously determined attitudinal set held by the therapist which interferes with his work" (Singer, 1970, p. 290). Countertransference can be worked through effectively with personal therapy, lab sessions, and active self-exploration. Beginning crisis intervention students have often experienced one or more of the situational crises practiced in coaching sessions. If students have not worked through the crisis completely, their feelings may interfere with their ability to remain calm, objective, and client focused. However, once students' unresolved issues are discovered and processed, both in their own counseling and in lab group, they often are able to work quite effectively with clients going through that same type of crisis. Countertransference is not restricted to students in training. In actuality, this concept was first developed by Sigmund Freud in his training of psychoanalysts. Even the highly trained professional is liable to experience countertransference from time to time. This is the primary reason that personal analysis has been encouraged for psychoanalysts from the very beginning of the discipline.

DUAL RELATIONSHIPS

Another ethical issue involves a **dual relationship**—that is, a counselor's having more than one kind of relationship with a client. When counselors are providing crisis intervention to a client, they should not be involved with that client on a personal level of any kind. This includes prohibition of any relationship—sexual, social, employment, or financial—that is not directly related to the provision of crisis intervention. Such a separation is necessary because a person in crisis is often in a vulnerable state and could be taken advantage of quite easily by a counselor (who is viewed as an expert). Another reason to avoid a dual relationship is because of the possible emotional damage clients may sustain if they experience the counselor in a different role and then are disillusioned or disappointed. Also, the power differential between counselor and client is enormous. The counselor knows quite a bit about the client, and this knowledge can be a source of awkwardness for the client when he or she is out of the therapeutic situation. The most potent word on the subject is this: *Don't make friends or lovers of your clients. It is unethical and in some cases illegal.*

CONFIDENTIALITY

Confidentiality is one of the hallmarks of any trusting relationship. It is also an important part of the ethical code for mental health providers. A broad concept that refers to safeguarding clients from unauthorized disclosures of information made in the therapeutic relationship, confidentiality is an explicit promise by the counselor to reveal nothing unless the client has agreed to it. **Privileged communication,** which is sometimes confused with confidentiality, is the statutory right that protects clients from having their confidences revealed publicly (Corey, Corey, & Callanan, 1993, pp. 102–103).

As they relate to crisis intervention, however, some exceptions to privilege and confidentiality do exist. Privilege is waived if the client signs a document giving the helper permission to disclose the communications between the client and the counselor. Clients may be asked to waive privilege to ensure continuity of care among mental health professionals, to provide for appropriate supervision, when access to records is needed for court testimony, and when information is needed for submitting health insurance claims. Confidentiality must be broken in cases of child abuse or elder abuse, when the client is a danger to self or others, and may be broken when a client is gravely disabled. Sometimes, a client's mental condition will be the focus of a lawsuit, and in some cases confidentiality can be ethically and legally broken. For example, a client who sues a therapist for malpractice and claims to have suffered emotional damage because of the therapist's incompetence gives up privilege to communications from the therapy sessions. The therapist may use case notes to defend against the malpractice charge. A similar example in which a client would forfeit the protection of privilege is a case in which the client is attempting to prove emotional injury in a workers' compensation lawsuit.

The other exceptions to confidentiality fit under the adage "Privileged communication ends where public peril begins." This includes peril to clients if they endanger themselves because of a mental disorder. If clients are considered suicidal or gravely disabled and unable to care for themselves, helpers may breach confidentiality to protect them. The spirit of this allowance is that sharing information is meant to be among professionals, family, and friends, and not for frivolous purposes. Gravely disabled clients are those who, because of a mental disorder, cannot take care of their daily needs for food, shelter, medical care, clothing, and so on. Clearly, it is more important to break confidentiality to save someone with Alzheimer's disease from starving because he is delusional about having food in the house than it is to maintain confidentiality.

The other situations in which privileged communications should be broken involve trying to prevent clients from harming others. These conditions include elder abuse, child abuse, and the possibility that clients might cause different kinds of danger to others.

Elder Abuse Reporting Act

The department of social services in some states has an adult protective services program that responds to reports of abuse of the elderly (i.e., adults over 65 years old). Elder abuse refers to any of the following acts inflicted by other than accidental means on an elder by another person: physical abuse, fiduciary abuse (involves trust and money), and neglect or abandonment. In many states, knowledge of such abuse must be reported to social services, the police, or a nursing home ombudsman (governmental investigator). Some agencies have also begun taking reports of abuse of the disabled adult population. This could cover any adult who suffers from a mental or physical disability such as mental retardation or blindness.

Child Abuse Reporting Act

Since passage by Congress of the National Child Abuse Prevention and Treatment Act in 1974, many states have enacted laws requiring professionals to report child abuse. States differ on the indicators for reporting and whether sanctions will be imposed on individuals for not reporting. According to most professional associations, protecting children from harm is an ethical obligation, and there is a growing trend to ensure that reporting professionals are given immunity from suit if the suspicion proves to be false (Corey, 1996, p. 179). Child abuse reporting includes suspicions of physical abuse, sexual abuse, general neglect, and emotional abuse.

In many states, child abuse must be reported within 36 hours of its discovery to the department of social services or the police. The child protective services program will then investigate the suspicion. Remember that as a mental health provider, you are not required to have evidence of abuse before you report; you need only the suspicion that it exists. If you suspect abuse that is later proved and you failed to report it, you may be fined by the state.

On the other hand, more and more states are ensuring immunity from suit for false reports.

The Tarasoff Case   The consequences of failing to warn an individual of possible danger to her or him by another are dramatically illustrated in the Tarasoff case. In 1969, Prosenjit Poddar was seeing a therapist at the campus counseling center of the University of California, Berkeley. Poddar confided to the therapist that he intended to kill Tatiana Tarasoff when she returned from Brazil. The therapist considered Poddar dangerous and called campus police, requesting that Poddar be confined. He was not confined. To complicate matters, the therapist's supervisor ordered that all case notes be destroyed. Tarasoff was later killed by Poddar, and her parents filed suit against the California Board of Regents. The decision from this case requires a therapist to notify the police and the intended victim when possible if the therapist has reasonable belief that a client is dangerous toward others (**duty to warn**) (Corey, Corey, & Callanan, 1993, pp. 117–119).

INFORMED CONSENT

Informed consent is a way of "providing clients with information they need to become active participants in the therapeutic relationship" (Corey, Corey, & Callanan, 1993, p. 87). Although no specific rules exist governing how much information a therapist is to provide, three legal elements to informed consent do exist. First, clinicians must make sure clients have the ability to make rational decisions and, if not, must ensure that a parent or guardian takes responsibility for giving consent. Second, therapists must give clients information in a clear way and check their understanding of the risks and benefits of treatment and alternate procedures available. Third, clients must consent freely to treatment. The exceptions to these elements occur when clients are dangerous to themselves and others or are gravely disabled. Electroconvulsive shock treatments and psychosurgery (lobotomies) cannot be done without consent; however, there are times when medication is given without client consent.

SUPERVISION AND TRAINING

The ethical code requiring counselors to receive appropriate supervision and training must be followed for both the benefit of the client and the clinician's growth and confidence. Unless paraprofessionals are supervised by a licensed professional, most agencies—county, state, and nonprofit—do not let them provide crisis intervention and counseling. Even seasoned therapists should consult with colleagues about cases for which they have minimal training or experience. Referring a client to another helper is often done by crisis workers because the worker's duties mainly involve assessment and brokering out clients—tasks requiring a sound knowledge of community resources for a variety of problems.

Being able to make an assessment for organic illnesses and severe mental illness is especially important when a helper is conducting a crisis interview. Some cases require a multidisciplinary team approach with medical doctor involvement; they must be identified if the patient is to receive the total help needed. Even though making technical diagnoses is not usually considered appropriate for paraprofessionals, knowledge of the *Diagnostic and Statistical Manual of Mental Disorders* (American Psychiatric Association, 1994) is helpful in ensuring that clients receive services from the type of professional appropriate to their needs. This manual provides information about very serious mental disorders that require intervention by physicians. Crisis workers should review this manual when possible to gain a beginning understanding of the types of presenting complaints that usually necessitate physician involvement.

> **Example:** Suppose that a 45-year-old woman comes to a community center because her 70-year-old mother has been behaving strangely, does not recognize her family members, and leaves the gas stove burners on all day. Knowing that these symptoms are indicative of Alzheimer's disease or other organic brain disorders helps the crisis worker develop treatment strategies. Most important is having the woman examined neurologically to rule out any medical cause for her unusual behavior.

BURNOUT AND SECONDARY POSTTRAUMATIC STRESS DISORDER

People who regularly work with individuals in crisis situations may be prone to develop symptoms of burnout, or what can be referred to as secondary posttraumatic stress disorder (PTSD), which will be covered in detail in Chapter 11.

Burnout has been studied by many and has been seen in a variety of workers throughout the nation. Crisis workers should be informed about the possible symptoms and causes of burnout to be able to identify this state in themselves. The causes, definitions, and prevention of burnout are discussed. Secondary PTSD is then discussed in the context of a research study conducted by the author with 67 community workers who deal with crisis situations daily.

Definitions of Burnout

Maslach & Jackson (1986) have proposed three dimensions of burnout. Lack of personal accomplishment, emotional exhaustion, and depersonalization and deindividuation of clients are often the reactions of workers to chronic stress. Burnout can be thought of as a "syndrome of physical and emotional exhaustion involving the development of negative self-concept, negative job attitudes, and a loss of concern and feelings for clients" (Pines & Maslach, 1978, p. 224). When these reactions occur, individuals in the helping professions who are particularly susceptible to burnout may develop negative and cynical attitudes and feelings toward clients and may not be as supportive as needed (Vettor & Kosinski, 2000, p. 1).

Symptoms of Burnout

Researchers have described a variety of physical and emotional symptoms indicative of burnout. In the 1980s, hundreds of workers at an aircraft manufacturing facility developed symptoms of burnout that were referred to as **aerospace syndrome**. Most suffered from dizziness, nausea, headaches, fatigue, palpitations, shortness of breath, and cognitive impairment. Three-fourths of them also showed symptoms of major depression and panic disorder (Sparks et al., 1990).

Other common symptoms of burnout include psychosomatic illness, social withdrawal, substance abuse, and deterioration of family and social relationships (Freudenberger, 1975; Maslach & Jackson, 1986).

Causes of Burnout

Negative emotional and behavioral reactions on the job occur in many professions. Human service workers may be more prone to burnout as a result of conflicts between an idealistic "professional mystique" and the harsh realities of working in human services (Leiter, 1991). In addition, human services workers may find it emotionally taxing when consumers resent them, when they must work with consumers with limited capabilities to help themselves, when they must deal with tedious bureaucratic exercises daily, and when they receive little positive feedback from authority figures (Gomez & Michaelis, 1995). Lack of company support, poor relations among staff, lack of competence, and a perception that success is unlikely on the job are other general causes of burnout (Clarke, 2000).

In helping professions in which the professionals such as emergency medical technicians (EMTs) must deal with intense emotional arousal, depersonalization is used to minimize this arousal. Burnout may be seen as a coping strategy to ensure that performance is not affected in these crisis situations. Burnout may also occur as part of a tendency for helping professionals to evaluate themselves negatively when assessing their work with patients (Vettor & Kosinski, 2000). EMTs may be more susceptible to burnout because they are faced with human tragedies such as as injury, mutilation, and death on a daily basis. Services are often delivered in a hostile world of darkness, poor weather conditions, difficult terrain, and unpredictable dangers (Vettor & Kosinski, 2000). The technicians are at risk for developing secondary PTSD from exposure to critical incidents. (Effects of exposure to critical incidents are discussed in detail in Chapter 11.)

Negative emotional and behavioral reactions have also been observed in professionals who are not considered to be in the helping professions but who deal with crisis situations. Aerospace syndrome was determined to be caused by several psychosocial aspects in the workplace. Fear of chemicals, labeling of aerospace syndrome, fear of AIDS, mass hysteria crisis building, work intensity, mental strain, increased production pressure, tense labor-management relations, inadequate attention to safety, and reinforcement of fear by media and coworkers were all found to be causes of high work-stress burnout among aerospace workers (Vettor & Kosinski, 2000). The mass hysteria was so extreme that only 14 of the hundreds of workers observed showed no symptoms!

Prevention of Burnout

Several conditions may help prevent burnout and increase positive emotional reactions among workers. Kruger, Bernstein, and Botman (1995) suggest that having fun with team members, work discussions, peer cohesion, and social support, in which assistance is directed toward helping the worker cope with stressful circumstances, combine to reduce symptoms of burnout.

Human services workers who spend more time in direct contact with consumers and less time processing paperwork had higher scores on personal accomplishment assessments (Gomez & Michaelis, 1995). Reduced feelings of personal accomplishment have been associated with burnout, so it appears that one way to reduce burnout would be to spend more time with clients. However, because paperwork is often required in human services occupations, management would be wise to ensure that workers have enough client contact, as this seems to buffer workers against the worst effects of stress and is a valuable source of reward among staff. Other factors that may reduce burnout include workers feeling that they have some control over their time at work, some control over their workload, and an ability to organize their own work. Recognition of quality of care is also helpful in reducing burnout, as is clarity over one's role at work.

A Study of Community Crisis Workers

Sixty-seven community workers were surveyed in 2001 by the author with the assistance of several of her students who collected data by personally distributing questionnaires to various community workers who frequently work with crisis situations. These workers responded to questions regarding their emotional and behavioral reactions to working with people in crisis. Emergency room physicians and nurses, ambulance drivers, mental health workers, rape crisis counselors, firefighters, and police were included. The types of crisis situations they commonly work with were also identified.

Of the 67 workers surveyed, 21 identified themselves as counselors or therapists, 12 as police officers, 3 as physicians, 11 as nurses, 5 as emergency response workers, 7 as firefighters, and 8 as "other."

Table 3.1 shows the types of crises dealt with according to occupation.

The participants were asked several questions about their reactions to working with people in crisis. When asked if they felt anxiety when a client reports being suicidal, 23 (34%) of the crisis workers said yes. Only 12 (17%) reported being depressed after working with a person in crisis. However, when asked if there had ever been times when the worker was unable to stop thinking about clients in crisis, 41 (64%) said yes. These problems do not seem to prevent workers from going to work, though, as only 4 participants (all counselors) said they had missed work as a result of working with people in crisis. There was little increase in drug or alcohol use reported as a result of working

TABLE 3.1 | TYPES OF CRISES DEALT
WITH BY OCCUPATION

Type of Crisis Situation	Counselor	Police	Physician	Nurse	Emergency Response Worker	Firefighter	Other
	N = 21	N = 12	N = 3	N = 11	N = 5	N = 7	N = 8
Medical	4	12	3	11	4	3	0
Sexual assault	12	7	1	8	3	5	6
Spousal abuse	17	8	2	7	2	6	7
Child abuse	19	7	1	7	2	6	4
Victim of robbery or burglary	1	3	0	7	1	5	1
Victim of physical assault	14	7	2	10	4	6	5
Significant other of a murder victim	1	3	0	4	1	5	0
Victim of a natural disaster	1	2	0	7	3	4	0
Victim of a shooting spree	1	3	1	7	3	3	0
Substance abuse crisis	6	11	3	9	3	5	3
Sexually transmitted disease, HIV, AIDS crisis	5	6	2	9	2	3	1
Teen runaway, pregnancy, disobedience	16	4	2	2	1	4	6
Disability crisis	5	9	2	8	3	2	2
Illness crisis	8	11	3	9	4	2	2

with crises. Only 5 people stated that their use increased. This low number does not mean that the workers do not feel stress. In response to the question about feeling powerless after working with people in crisis, 23 (34%) answered that they did. This same percentage stated that they felt grouchy or agitated after dealing with people in crisis.

One common response of workers who deal with crises seems to be anger at the system. Thirty (45%) stated feeling angry at the system when working with someone in crisis. It is no wonder then that 35 (52%) of the workers stated that they think of quitting their job one to five times a month.

As to what these workers do when feeling emotionally stressed after working with people in crisis, the vast majority (80%) stated they talk with coworkers. Only 13 (19%) stated that they seek professional mental health services when feeling emotionally stressed.

The results of this study and previously discussed ones indicate that workers have many emotional, psychological, and behavioral reactions to stressful working conditions. In the case of crisis workers, many of the symptoms reported in this study are similar to the types of symptoms found in people going through a crisis. Symptoms of posttraumatic stress disorder included the inability to stop thinking about the client in crisis, agitation, irritability, anxiety, depression, and thoughts of wanting to quit the job. Because these symptoms are a result of working with people going through a crisis and not the result of the workers' own personal crises, it can be thought of as **secondary PTSD.**

The fact that these symptoms were reported to exist by so many of the crisis workers surveyed indicates a need for a strategy to reduce these symptoms. As was shown in many of the studies presented earlier as well as in the responses of this current study, maintaining ongoing communication with coworkers is essential in managing the symptoms. It is hoped that this will allow crisis workers to stay on the job at peak effectiveness.

KEY TERMS FOR STUDY

burnout: Feelings and behaviors that often result when a crisis worker feels powerless to help people in crisis. Symptoms of burnout include absenteeism, agitation, depression, anxiety, and anger.

child abuse reporting: Reporting required of anyone working with children as a counselor, doctor, teacher, or any other capacity since passage of the 1974 Child Abuse Prevention and Treatment Act by Congress. These people must report any suspicions of child abuse to the child protective services agency in their state. The requirement is mandatory and in many states overrides the client's right to confidentiality.

confidentiality: An ethical standard providing the client with the right for all disclosures in counseling to be kept private.

countertransference: A situation in a counseling relationship that arises from unresolved feelings experienced by a counselor in a session with a client. These feelings come out of the counselor's personal life and cause him or her to act out these feelings with a client, behavior that may cause emotional harm to the client.

danger to others: Condition in which a client is deemed to be a threat to others. At this time, the counselor must breach confidentiality and report his or her concerns to the police or the intended victim, or both. This is called the "duty to warn."

dual relationship: A relationship that a counselor engages in with the client outside the professional one—for example, a social, sexual, or business relationship.

elder abuse: Physical abuse, fiduciary abuse, neglect, or abandonment of someone 65 years old or older. In many states, anyone working with clients over 65 years of age must report suspected cases of elder abuse to the state's adult protective services agency. This reporting is often mandatory and grounds for breaching confidentiality.

exceptions to privilege and confidentiality: Situations in which communications between therapist and client can be legally and ethically shared with others. In the case of confidentiality, these include elder abuse and child abuse; when the client is gravely disabled; and when the client is a danger to self or others. In the case of privilege, these include voluntary waivers given by the client for information to be shared in a limited forum as well as some involuntary disclosure, as in certain court cases.

gravely disabled: Condition in which clients are psychotic or suffering from a severe organic brain disorder. People with such disorders are often incapable of meeting basic needs, such as obtaining food or shelter and managing finances. Being gravely disabled is often a reason for involuntary hospitalization of a person.

informed consent: Permission for treatment given by a client to a therapist after the client has been thoroughly informed about all aspects of the treatment. Anyone entering a counseling relationship has the right to understand the nature of therapy, give his or her consent for it, understand that it is voluntary, and be told the limits of confidentiality.

mental status exam: An examination used to rule out severe forms of mental illness and organic disorders. As part of their ethical responsibility, crisis interventionists must know when to refer a client to a physician. Use of this exam can help in making those determinations.

privilege: The legal counterpart of confidentiality. Clients may waive the right to privilege if they wish the counselor to share certain information in court or other limited venues.

4 | CHAPTER

CULTURAL SENSITIVITY IN CRISIS INTERVENTION

Interest in the sensitivity of counselors and therapists to culturally diverse clients has been growing in the past few decades. It began in the 1960s when the civil rights and affirmative action movements emerged, and became a part of formal education in the late 1980s and 1990s. Arredondo and colleagues (1996, p. 43) describe specific behaviors and attitudes of culturally aware counselors: "Multicultural counseling refers to preparation and practices that integrate multicultural and culture-specific awareness, knowledge, and skills into counseling interactions." They suggest that **multicultural** refers to five major cultural groups in the United States: African Americans, Asian Americans, Caucasians, Latinos, and Native Americans. The reader is encouraged to obtain a copy of their article and keep it for reference. Although these groups have been the main focus of multicultural studies, other subgroups such as people with disabilities; gays, lesbians, bisexuals, and transgenders; and certain religious groups also have special needs.

This chapter explores the process of becoming a culturally sensitive counselor. Additionally, special issues and intervention strategies related to working with various ethnic groups, persons with disabilities, and gays and lesbians are discussed.

DEVELOPMENT OF CULTURALLY SENSITIVE PSYCHOTHERAPISTS

As part of a course in a doctoral program at the University of Southern California, seven students coauthored an article that describes the development of cultural sensitivity in therapists. The

13

TABLE 4.1 | PROPOSED STAGES AND STATE-SPECIFIC CONSEQUENCES IN THERAPISTS' DEVELOPMENT OF CULTURAL SENSITIVITY

Stage	Description	Consequence
Unawareness of cultural issues	Therapist does not consider a cultural hypothesis in diagnosis.	Therapist does not understand the significance of the clients' cultural background to their functioning.
Heightened awareness of culture	Therapist is aware that cultural factors are important in fully understanding clients.	Therapist feels unprepared to work with culturally different clients; frequently applies own perception of clients' cultural background and therefore fails to understand the cultural significance for a specific client; can at times accurately recognize the influence of clients' cultural background on their functioning.
Burden of considering culture	Therapist is hypervigilant in identifying cultural factors and is, at times, confused in determining the cultural significance of clients' actions.	Therapist believes that consideration of culture is perceived as detracting from his or her clinical effectiveness.
Movement toward cultural sensitivity	Therapist entertains cultural hypotheses and carefully tests these hypotheses from multiple sources before accepting cultural explanations.	Therapist has increased likelihood of accurately understanding the role of culture on clients' functioning.

Source: Lopez et al. (1989). ©1989 by the American Psychological Association. Adapted with permission.

students and their professor found similar patterns as all of them struggled with the gender and ethnic issues involved in diagnosing and treating various groups. Based on case vignettes and class discussion, a model of developmental stages was created and is shown in Table 4.1. Counselors do not have to be perfect models of cultural sensitivity, but they do need to be aware of cultural, ethnic, religious, and gender issues that may affect the crisis intervention process.

Knowing about various cultures before meeting with clients can be helpful. It is more important, however, to follow a client's lead in these matters, in order to help the client feel understood and validated. If a counselor fails to respect cultural differences, the crisis intervention may come to an end. In the following case example, the therapist did not show cultural sensitivity, with the consequence that the client dropped out of therapy prematurely.

> **Example:** A 41-year-old man requested an emergency session regarding his marriage. At his request, I saw him Saturday morning. The man spoke with an Asian accent and said that he was half-Chinese and half-Spanish and had been born in China. As we discussed his presenting problem, the client resisted any of my suggestions that part of his problem might be that his wife was Caucasian and her parents and siblings disapproved of him. He had come to my office to appease his wife, who said she would leave him unless he sought counseling. The couple had a poor sex life, but he resisted discussing this openly. He kept insisting that the problem was him, and he described himself as a cold person who did not like to be around people.
>
> I noticed myself becoming very frustrated. The client refused to accept the idea that he and his wife had a relationship problem. I guess the client sensed my frustration because he asked if I could refer him to another therapist. He had many demands regarding the times he was available for appointments. He refused marital therapy, which I recommended. I guessed that some of his issues were cultural in nature, but, unfortunately, I will not have the opportunity to explore these issues with him. (Lopez et al., 1989, p. 370)
>
> This vignette indicated that the therapist did not consider cultural factors in her work with this ethnic minority client. She appears to be defining the problem for the client without considering the client's definition of the problem and working from there. This is not to say that the therapist is wrong in her assessment; the client is likely having marital problems. However, her failure to validate his explanatory model or interpretation of the problem may have led to his request for another therapist. (Lopez et al., 1989, p. 371)

The intent of this chapter is to teach readers how to look at certain groups so they can form a working model that will help them understand the norms and family structures of the groups, crises that often arise, and interventions that will alleviate them.

LATINOS

The terms *Hispanic, Latino,* and *of Spanish descent* all refer to people whose culture was influenced by the Spanish conquerors of the 15th and 16th centuries. Most of these Spaniards settled in Central and South America. **Hispanic** is an umbrella term for descendants of the colonized natives, Hispanos, and descendants of foreigners and political and economic refugees. **Latino** refers to people from Latin America, which is actually Central and South America. Although there are differences between the various Latino groups, certain similarities exist as well. The most notable commonality is the Spanish language. Language influences thoughts and behaviors, and, therefore, many Latino groups have similar customs. The Spanish influence is also evident in many of their cultural patterns.

About 35.3 million Latinos reside in the United States. They are by far the largest minority group (U.S. Bureau of the Census, 2001). They range from Mexican Americans to Puerto Rican Americans to Cuban Americans to Central and South Americans. Over 10 million live in California, a state that borders Mexico and was at one time a territory of Mexico. Many Mexican traditions are alive and well in the coastal state. About 6.6 million Latinos live in Texas, and about 2.8 million in New York. Florida has 2.6 million, Illinois 1.5 million, and Arizona 1.2 million. New Mexico is home to 765,386, which is 42% of the total population of the state. Because Mexican Americans are the largest group of Latinos in the United States (about 58.5% of all Latinos), it is important to examine Mexican American culture. Counselors should use information about this culture when conducting crisis intervention. Despite differences in migration patterns and other historical events, most Latino individuals have been strongly influenced by their Spanish heritage, so the issues discussed are relevant for other Latinos as well as Mexican Americans.

Mexican American Families

Over 20.6 million Mexican Americans live in the United States. They often suffer discrimination in housing, employment, and education. Their school dropout rate is high, and they are often exploited by employers, who keep them in low-paying, low-prestige jobs. They often do not receive welfare benefits despite their high unemployment rate. The "oppressed servant mentality" that was forced on them after they were conquered by the Spaniards is still evident in their lives. Mexicans who emigrate to California or other states usually do so because they are poor. They want to earn enough money to survive and also support their families back in Mexico.

Most Mexicans are *mestizo* people, who have a mixed American Indian and Spanish heritage. From the 17th century to the 19th century, Spain extended its rule over the region that is now Mexico and moved into California and other southwestern states. The Spaniards and Indians shared much, but the Spaniards took Mexico's riches and kept the natives poor. Spanish priests taught Catholicism to the natives, who combined it with their own religions. From these interchanges, a new culture was created: the Mexican culture.

After the 1848 gold rush in California, settlers from the eastern part of the United States went west, and conflicts began to erupt between them and the Mexicans. The two groups lived separately. Eventually, Mexicans lost much of their property and many of their rights to the newcomers. The U.S. citizens were happy to settle in areas where gold could be mined and other natural resources such as agricultural land and water were available. The Mexicans were pushed far back into Mexico, where the land is arid and not suitable for agriculture. Industrial development has been slow in Mexico, and it has become a poor country (McGoldrick, Pearce, & Giordana, 1982).

Many Mexicans stayed in the United States. Areas in which they settled, creating pockets of their own subculture, are sometimes called **barrios.** Some Mexican Americans speak English and have adopted some mainstream values, but they still have certain distinctive values. Because the United States and

Mexico are so close to each other geographically, Mexicans continue to enter the United States illegally. The undocumented status of many Mexicans is an important factor in understanding their behavior. Sensitivity to the history of Mexican American clients can help crisis counselors approach them with empathy.

Mexican American Cultural Patterns

One Mexican cultural behavior that may differ from Anglo norms is child-rearing practices. In Anglo-American culture, autonomy is stressed; in Mexican culture, however, nurturance and obedience to authority are stressed. Mexican American children often appear to be delayed developmentally. For example, a 5-year-old may sit on his mother's lap; a 3-year-old may drink out of a bottle; and a 14-year-old may spend all her time with her mother. However, these behaviors are all considered normal in Mexican American culture.

Physical distance between people is another difference. By Anglo standards, Mexican Americans might seem overinvolved with, enmeshed with, or overprotective of one another. It is normal, however, for family members to sit close together or to assume that they are to be included in any individual family member's crisis (McGoldrick, Pearce, & Giordana, 1982, p. 151). Because family closeness is such an important part of Latino culture, crisis workers should keep systems theory in mind when working with Mexican American families.

> **Example:** If an 18-year-old daughter is raped or a 22-year-old daughter battered, it is likely that each young woman's family will become involved in helping her through the crisis. This is not to say they will tell her to leave her husband or go to trial for the rape. The daughter will most likely tell them of her distress, however. In many Anglo cultures, victims deal with these crises with the help of professionals and community support groups without telling their families about their problems.

Mexican American families sometimes do not seek help because they do not know about community resources (McGoldrick, Pearce, & Giordana, 1982, p. 154). Language barriers, racism, or lack of knowledge may keep them from using even the most basic services available. Workers should not try to conduct long-term introspective, psychodynamic psychotherapy (which, by the way, is counter to most Mexican American norms). Instead, workers should serve as "brokers" for services. This is often an extremely helpful role for a counselor who is working with a Mexican American family in crisis.

> **Example:** In some families, the children are bilingual but a parent speaks only Spanish. Children may not get the services they need because the parents feel embarrassed or frustrated when they try to explain their needs to professionals and agencies. Often, the job of a crisis worker is to make contact with a school official or a legal advocacy program and connect a family with these services.

Personalismo is a cultural pattern of relating to others in a manner that may include exaggerated warmth and emotions and a strong need for rapport in order to feel safe or trust others. It is particularly important for crisis workers to grasp this concept when working with Latinos because developing trust is a hallmark process in the helping relationship. Workers may have to spend time in seemingly idle chitchat. The Latino culture is much more relationship oriented than task oriented, unlike mainstream American culture.

One last characteristic of Latinos is their tendency toward emotionalism, even exaggerated expression that borders on the dramatic. If given the chance and if they feel safe, they often express their feelings openly in counseling. This expression of affect may allow them to master their feelings. Caplan discussed this process when he proposed seven characteristics of people coping effectively. At times, crisis workers may just want to allow clients to express their feelings and not pressure them to solve a problem.

Issues Related to Different Rates of Acculturation

Other crises that may emerge in Mexican American families may reflect patterns that developed and were functional when the family first immigrated to the United States but have since become restrictive for certain family members. For example, many parents depend on their children to be their intermediaries with the larger culture. When the children grow up and want to separate from their parents, the parents may find it difficult to let them go (McGoldrick, Pearce, & Giordana, 1982, p. 155).

Adolescents may adopt Anglo values that are contrary to traditional Mexican values. Rejection of parents' cultural values may precipitate a crisis between an adolescent and a Mexican American mother or father.

> **Example:** A 15-year-old girl may act out rebelliously by dating boys, staying out late, or dressing less than modestly. A crisis interventionist may suggest that the parents take a more active role in their daughter's growing up by structuring traditional activities for her, such as a *quincinera* (a party to announce entrance to womanhood). The girl's acting-out behavior can then be reframed as confusion about whether she is growing up. A structured ritual will help everyone to more easily accept role changes and should help reduce the family's distress. (McGoldrick, Pearce, & Giordana, 1982, p. 156)

A teenager who joins a gang is acting in a way that is related to different rates of acculturation. In order not to accept an "oppressed servant mentality," the adolescent engages in the power and control activities that are common in gangs, such as drug dealing, drug use, assault, and murder. Gang activity may be considered a sign of negative acculturation of teenage Mexican Americans.

Using negotiation skills and finding compromises is essential for the interventionist working with dual-culture families. Remember that the parents have chosen to live in the United States; this decision says something about their desire to be connected with some parts of American culture. A counselor can weave this idea into positive reframing, pointing out the opportunity afforded the family that adopts certain Anglo behavioral norms. Studies have shown that emotional distress is higher in Latinos who have either adopted American cultural norms in toto or have held onto traditional Mexican cultural norms in toto (Hovey, 2000; McQueen, Getz, & Bray, 2003). Maintaining a bicultural identity seems to be the healthiest mental position for Latinos, and it should be encouraged by mental health clinicians.

Comparison of Mainstream Cultural Values and Latino Resistance in the Mental Health Field

Most theories and techniques in the counseling profession developed within an Anglo-Saxon value system. The three major camps that have traditionally defined mental health and emotional dysfunction are the behavioral, psychoanalytic, and humanistic systems. If crisis workers depend on these traditional theories when working with Latinos, they may encounter much resistance. Table 4.2 presents traditional mainstream values as related to these traditional models and possible Latino resistance to them.

Although these traditional approaches do not appear to be applicable to the Latino population, approaches do exist that are more amenable to their needs. In a 2000 research study (Kanel), 268 Latinos were asked what type of mental health services they would prefer. Of the individuals surveyed, 163 were low-skilled factory workers, most of whom spoke little English. The other 105 individuals were students at a local community college who were learning English or fulfilling general education requirements. The vast majority said they would seek out a counselor if they had family problems (67.2%) or if they had their own emotional problems (63.1%). Depression and nervousness were the problems for which they would be most likely to seek help (26.9% and 24.3%, respectively). Other problems that would precipitate a visit to a counselor included "out-of-control anger" (17.2%); marriage problems (18.7%); disobedient children (16%); anxiety (15.3%); children's school issues (15.3%); and drug problems (15.4%).

When asked about the way they would want the counselor to relate to them, 35.8% said they would prefer to have the counselor give a lot of advice, 26.5% stated they wanted the counselor to ask a lot of questions; 21.6% preferred the counselor to be personal; and 50.4% wanted the counselor to be very professional. Interestingly, although 63.8% believed that talking about their childhood would help resolve current problems, only 18.3% stated they would want to talk about their childhood; 66.4% preferred to talk about current problems. As for the use of medication, 59% did not believe it could help them with their problems, and only 7.8% preferred to take medication to resolve emotional problems.

The author simultaneously surveyed 43 Spanish-speaking therapists in southern California on their treatment of this population. When asked about the type of intervention they use with Spanish-speaking clients, 28% said cognitive-behavioral therapy, 26% said family counseling, 23% said psychoeducational therapy, and 23% said referrals to other agencies. These approaches in combination are the same as the crisis intervention model presented in this book.

Based on these results and Latino cultural norms, it appears that two approaches would be most effective: the family system model and the crisis intervention model (which is heavily influenced by cognitive, behavioral, and psychoeducational models).

Ataque de Nervios

One Latino phenomenon that may come to the crisis worker's attention is *ataque de nervios (los nervios),* which literally means "attack of nerves." This is

TABLE 4.2 | COMPARISON OF MAINSTREAM AND LATINO VALUES IN THE MENTAL HEALTH FIELD

Mainstream Theoretical Model	Latino Resistance
Behavioral Approaches to Parenting	
Behavior modification:	
a. Positive reinforcement or rewards	*Respeto:* Children should do what parents tell them to just because they are children.
b. Response cost	Punishment is considered a form of love and a way to avoid spoiling children.
c. Active parenting approach	Indirect, guilt-inducing methods are commonly used with teens; parenting is not active but assumed.
d. Plan for future parenting	Deal with parenting when it comes; present orientation.
Psychoanalytic Approaches to Parenting	
Stages of development move from complete dependence to complete independence:	
a. Complete dependence	Complete dependence lasts as long as possible.
b. First independence, mobility, self-feeding, bowel control	Physically: Some children are bottle-fed or nursed until they are 5 years old; even preschoolers may be hand-fed.
c. Social independence	Socially: Children have few friends outside the home; they play with siblings and cousins. Children do not have sleepovers. Intrafamilial dependence is normal.
d. Moral independence	Morally: Law and order are valued; children should do what authority says; they are not encouraged to make decisions on their own.
e. Emotional independence	Emotionally: Interdependence with parents and enmeshed boundaries are normal; children are expected to meet their parents' needs.
Humanistic and Existential Approaches to Parenting	
a. Self-awareness	Denial of relational conflicts; anxiety with self-awareness
b. Confrontation in relational conflicts	Avoidance of confrontation
c. Genuine encounters and intimacy	Lack of intimacy and authentic relating; interactions are prescribed and based on hierarchy and gender roles.

This table is the original work of Kanel, 2003.

a culture-bound, self-labeled syndrome found only in Latinos. It is often a reaction to trauma, death, marital infidelity, or family conflict. A person suffering from this may seek help from a physician, counselor, or *curandero* (folk healer). Symptoms include panic attacks, fits of violent agitation with self-mutilation and suicidal behavior (Schechter et al., 2000, p. 530), shaking, heart palpitations, numbness, shouting, swearing, striking others, falling, convulsions (Liebowitz et al., 1994, p. 871), and signs of dissociation (Oquendo, 1995).

In 2004, the author conducted a study of 198 Latinos whose dominant language was Spanish and 37 mental health clinicians who treat Spanish-speaking clients to better understand *ataque de nervios* and treat it. Mental health counselors have been confused about how best to diagnose this disorder and how to intervene when it occurs. The two main symptoms reported by participants were screaming and despair. Being out of control, crying, and feeling irritable and anxious were mentioned frequently as well. Crisis workers may attribute these symptoms to panic disorder, generalized anxiety disorder, or depression. Of the Latinos surveyed, 76% reported symptoms of *ataque de nervios* that could fit more than two diagnoses or would not fit any diagnosis. Others have reported confusion in diagnosing *ataque de nervios* when using the universally accepted nomenclature of the DSM-IV, developed by the American Psychiatric Association in 1994. None of those studies resulted in an exact fit with traditional diagnoses, either, and most recommended further study to better understand the relationships between *ataque de nervios* and other disorders (Koss-Chioino, 1999; Liebowitz et al., 1994; Oquendo, 1995; Schechter et al., 2000).

What then are the implications for the crisis worker when a client presents with *ataque de nervios?* Both groups in the author's 2004 study overwhelmingly selected family conflicts (76% of Latinos and 82% of clinicians) as the number one cause. Emotional problems and work conflicts were mentioned as the next two causes by the Latino group. Clinicians reported that drug and alcohol abuse, childhood abuse, and intrapsychic conflict were also important causes. Only 26% of clinicians stated that the cause was a biochemical imbalance. This is important information because people suffering from *ataque de nervios* are usually diagnosed as having biochemical imbalances and given medication as the treatment of choice. According to the study, however, the causes are interpersonal and psychological and, therefore, need psychological treatment and family therapy. Although medication may help, it is not sufficient. In fact, *curanderos* may help clients more than therapists if clients believe in the power of herbal cleansing or faith healing.

When Latinos present with *ataque de nervios,* crisis workers would be wise to use the ABC model, giving the client plenty of time to express feelings. Helping the client feel understood is vital for him or her to overcome the sense of being out of control. Family sessions are helpful. The focus should be on developing new ways to cope with stress in relation to family members and co-workers. If the symptoms are extremely debilitating, referral to a physician may be warranted. In the study, 31% of Latinos stated that they talked to family and friends to overcome *ataque de nervios,* 21% saw a therapist, 21% received medication from a physician, 17% said the condition went away by itself, 12% received medication from a psychiatrist, 10% saw a *curandero,* and 14% used folk remedies such as smelling onions, prayer, and hands-on healing. Of the clinicians surveyed, 60% used cognitive therapy, 56% supportive therapy, and 48% family therapy; 43% recommended using medication; and only 0.08% used expressive or psychoanalytic therapy.

AFRICAN AMERICAN FAMILIES

In an ideal world, people would pay no attention to skin color. However, if mental health providers do not realize that African American culture differs in various ways from mainstream American culture, they may do a disservice to this group. Even if one is not a bigot or does not discriminate against African Americans, one must understand the ways in which an African American person in crisis may be affected by racial issues.

When one considers the history of African Americans, one can understand their family structure and value systems. African Americans who were raised in slavery learned to exist in settings where roles were flexible and families usually extended to several generations. These aspects can be readily seen in modern-day African American families. Elderly people as well as young adults "tend to be supported by the collective efforts of family members both within and outside the nuclear family" (McGoldrick, Pearce, & Giordana, 1982, p. 90). This history certainly has implications for the crisis interventionist. The worker should use naturally existing support systems for each individual. The worker should also explore the role norms of the person's family system so he or she does not see a problem when none exists.

> **Example:** A child may be brought in by his parents for misbehaving in school. You may discover that the parents do not understand his behavior and seem to be ineffective in eliminating it. Perhaps the child's grandmother is perceived by all to be the primary disciplinarian and nurturer. Instead of taking those responsibilities away from the grandmother and giving them to the parents (which would disengage the grandmother from the problem), you may want to bring the grandmother into the sessions and work with her alongside the parents. You would be culturally biased if you insisted that only the parents be involved in the child's therapy.

Role of Religion in African American Life

Slaves found solace in the view that God would provide a better world for them after they had left this world of suffering. This tradition of strong religious beliefs and practices has been passed down through the generations and must be kept in mind by the crisis worker.

The church has been a forum in which many African American women and men have expressed their talents and leadership skills (McGoldrick, Pearce, & Giordana, 1982, p. 96) and have found a kind of haven from a racist society. For the crisis interventionist, incorporating the church into therapy, either by seeking support from a minister or by encouraging the client to become involved in church activities, is valuable. Many African Americans do not place much trust in mainstream, middle-class mental health counselors. African American ministers, however, often do trust counselors and may be able to allay the fears of parishioners who would benefit from counseling.

Sometimes, appeals for help from the church are not productive. If clients are extremely mistrustful of counselors, workers should not try to convince them to change their views. Instead, counselors can empathize with the distrust and help clients engage with traditional cultural support systems that they do trust, such as family and friends. Unfair treatment of African Americans by the legal system is well documented; a disturbing encounter with the system is one event that may lead to a family crisis.

Problem-Solving Model for African Americans

Not all African American families in crisis need to be referred to traditional support systems. A growing number have adopted mainstream, middle-class values and will respond to crisis intervention. Focusing on the presenting problems and setting up goal-specific plans often work well. Some African Americans will seek out and accept insight-oriented therapy. The most important goal is to determine the needs of a particular client or family and meet these needs with cultural sensitivity. The worker must always acknowledge that racism is present in our society and must try to understand the world of a client who deals with racism every day.

Wright (1993) emphasizes the importance of cultural sensitivity when a worker has an African American male client who is dealing with issues of sexual behavior and the risk of HIV infection or AIDS. His research shows that African American men may have different views about sexual categories and behavior than mainstream white men. AIDS is widespread among African Americans and is primarily spread by men. Therefore, intervention strategies must be sensitive to the values and behaviors of African American men.

Wright suggests that current educational materials, health facilities, and community-based AIDS education and prevention programs are inadequate in their cultural and racial sensitivity. He states that "the AIDS epidemic is not merely a medical dilemma but is a socio-cultural medical dilemma. For African American men, AIDS has become an overwhelming and devastating blow that has torn away at their already threatened health and social status" (Wright, 1993, p. 430). Wright recommends that future policies should address cultural issues when programs are created to help prevent and reduce the risk of AIDS transmission among African Americans.

Although this research focuses on social policy, individual crisis workers can also benefit from these studies of the sexual behavior of African American men. Crisis workers must realize that for this group, a person's sexual behavior does not necessarily cause the person to be labeled a homosexual, heterosexual, or bisexual. Asking questions such as "Are you gay?" to see if a person is at risk for AIDS would be inappropriate, because even though a man may be engaging in homosexual behavior, he may not regard himself as a homosexual. (This is true for any client, not just African American clients.) It would be more suitable to identify specific behaviors that are associated with a high risk of AIDS and to provide information about such behaviors and about ways to prevent transmission of the HIV virus. (See Chapter 9 for more details.) Once a worker understands the client's perspective, the worker has accomplished the most important part of his or her task. Using this knowledge to help the person cope is the next challenge.

ASIAN AMERICAN FAMILIES

Asian American families have their roots in East Asia—China, Japan, and Korea—which is an area distinguished by having the oldest continually recorded civilization in the world. Its history gives it a background very different from that of the West in a variety of ways. For example, there are differences in philosophical approaches to life that are dictated in the East by Confucianism and Buddhism rather than Judeo-Christianity. Eastern systems do not stress independence and autonomy but rather emphasize the importance of the family and the specific hierarchical roles established for all members. Rules for behavior are extremely strong and more formalized than in other cultures. Because these people lived for years under oppressive dynastic rule and needed to maintain a large labor force capable of heavy manual and agricultural labor, male offspring became more valued than female offspring (McGoldrick, Pearce, & Giordana, 1982, pp. 208–210).

There are historical differences between the various Asian cultures. Language is one difference; another is the specific immigration problems and circumstances that each group experienced. Many Vietnamese people fled in boats to escape Communist rule. Many Japanese people came to America to take advantage of financial investments and employment opportunities.

Crisis Intervention Issues for Asian Americans

Although not all persons of Asian descent react the same, certain characteristics are commonly seen in people in crisis states and those using coping skills. The typical middle-class Judeo-Christian attitude of many mainstream training programs and work settings in the mental health field often does not address the special needs of Asian Americans.

The idea that the family should be placed ahead of individuals is one cultural difference that can definitely affect the counselor's work. Asian Americans are traditionally taught to respect family needs more than personal needs. Kashiwagi (1993, p. 46) states that "back in the old country the people had to band together, work together cooperatively, just to survive. I think because this value system worked then it was handed down." He further proposes that Asians who came to America felt the need to prove themselves, and this set up the "model minority" stereotype. This tradition of being overachieving, hardworking, and industrious may lead to stress and pressure to maintain the status quo inside and outside the Asian American community. The crisis worker should keep these characteristics in mind when working with this population.

Southeast Asians and Posttraumatic Stress Disorder

Kinzie and his colleagues (1984) have noted certain values held by Southeast Asian clients that affect the course of psychotherapy when they are treated for posttraumatic stress disorder (PTSD):

1. An orientation to the past, including great respect for ancestors
2. A primary reliance on the family as the basis of personal identity and self-esteem
3. The tolerance of multiple belief systems in regard to religion and cosmology and acceptance of life as it is rather than what it could be (pp. 645–646)

The mainstream-oriented crisis worker must consider these values when dealing with this Asian population so as not to force values on them that do not fit with their cultural norms. However, Boehnlein (1987, p. 525) believes that the mainstream cognitive psychotherapeutic approach does have relevance for Cambodian patients with PTSD:

> This approach facilitates an ongoing dialogue allowing the therapist to directly address issues in treatment that may relate to conflicting beliefs and values, along with doubts about one's personal and social identities that may affect interpersonal functioning. This is especially helpful in PTSD patients who have such profound doubts about their self-worth and their abilities to make effective changes in their lives based on personal traumatic histories and religious belief systems which often lead to a pessimistic view of fate.

Boehnlein (1987, p. 526) offers some specific questions a crisis worker might ask a Southeast Asian client with PTSD:

> "Do you have to attain perfection in order to not consider yourself a failure?"
> "Given the progress you have steadily been making, is your life still fated to be continuously and forever difficult?"
> "You have been viewing yourself as a weak and ineffective person, yet you had the strength as an adolescent to survive years of starvation and brutality. There must be strengths that you and your family possess that you have not been aware of in recent years." [Note that these statements are examples of reframing.]

Boehnlein further notes that these patients tend to minimize outward emotional expression. Persons with PTSD who feel they must not display emotions can use up a lot of psychic energy. Therefore, when working with Asian patients with PTSD, crisis workers need to be aware of their own affective responses and the subtle cues of internal distress communicated by patients. These cues may be communicated through reports of dreams or perhaps behavioral signs of depression, such as somatic distress or sleep disturbance.

Finally, Boehnlein (p. 527) suggests that the

> therapist can communicate a sense of warmth, genuineness, and competence by being direct, yet compassionate; by being assertive in the recommendation of treatment approaches, yet responsive to possibly conflicting cultural concepts of illness and healing; and by allowing the patient to report difficult historical information or express intense emotion without a sense of shame. Explaining to patients in a matter-of-fact way that a number of their experiences and feelings are shared by many other Cambodians does not trivialize their personal situation but instead serves to minimize their fear of going crazy.

This is a good example of how educational comments and reframing can be used.

In his work with Asian Americans, Hong (1988) has found that mental health workers would do well to adopt a general family practice model whereby they maintain an ongoing interaction with the family and serve as a resource that the family can consult when they are in difficulty. A counselor should use knowledge of the client as well as knowledge of the client's family, community, and social environment. This approach seems particularly suitable for Asian Americans whose culture emphasizes the role of the family. It helps to minimize the client's inhibition against seeking mental health services, gives the client the advantage of having family support, and helps the client in therapy because there is less resistance from the family system.

Whenever possible, the crisis worker must take into consideration the effect any intervention will have on the client's family. The worker should bring in the family whenever possible. To suggest that a client focus exclusively on her or his own problems will undoubtedly wreak havoc on the family system.

> **Example:** A 26-year-old Vietnamese female came for crisis intervention because of her depression and the increasing tension in her house. She was a medical student and working full-time. Her father expected her to serve him, support the family financially, and stay at home when she was not at school or work. Her older brother was permitted to lie around the house, contributing nothing; the client was very angered by this inequality. She realized that she had become quite Anglicized in her value system and felt taken advantage of by her family. She was miserable and pondered suicide.

In analyzing this case, the helper realized that cultural sensitivity was vital. If the counselor thought only in terms of middle-class, Caucasian values, he would support the separation/individuation process and encourage the client to assert her own needs and rights. However, if this client were to go against the wishes of her father, she would be ostracized from her family. A few concepts can help explain this dilemma.

Asian American Family Structure

In most traditional Asian families, males are respected more than females. The oldest son has more privileges than his own mother, though he must respect her at certain levels. The mother plays the stereotypical role of nurturer, providing domestic structure, whereas the father dictates all family decisions. The daughter contributes to the household until she marries; then she belongs to her husband's household and family. The concept of individualism is not part of this culture.

Shame and Obligation in Asian American Culture

If the norms are not followed, an individual and the family will experience a sense of shame, not only for their own actions but for the entire family line. This factor makes it necessary at times to reject a family member completely so as not to bring shame on the family. Differentiation between the family as a whole and its members often does not exist as it does in European cultures. Obligation arises in any situation in which the rules of family structure come into play. The child is obligated to respect the structure. If the child does not, he or she will bring shame on the family. Having to choose between obligation and individual freedom often brings on feelings of depression and anxiety. The crisis worker needs to be sensitive to these struggles and search for ways to negotiate compromises when possible.

In the case of the young medical student, the counselor did not suggest that she move out and tell her father that she is an adult and does not have to support him. Instead, the counselor encouraged her to use the counseling sessions as times to vent her frustrations. The crisis worker let the young woman know that she understood her dilemma and that by choosing to maintain the status quo, the woman could continue to be a part of her family. The consequences for violating the system would be complete alienation from her mother and sisters as well as the men in her family. If she could learn to keep her focus on the value of family, perhaps she could learn to let go of her feelings of unfairness. In reframing the situation, the worker pointed out that although the client felt a lot of pressure to keep the family from being shamed, her father felt this obligation even more. In actuality, the father carried the burden of keeping his family in line. He would experience incredible shame if his daughter were to move out while she was unmarried and refuse to support his family financially.

Kashiwagi (1993, p. 46) provides another example of how "certain traditional Asian cultural influences, such as bringing shame to the family and losing face in the community," have an effect on mental health problems and intervention. He asserts that when an Asian American teenager has a drug or alcohol addiction, the family often denies the condition and perpetuates the problem. This denial results in large part from the lack of connection, communication, and understanding in the parent-child relationship. If the counselor recommends a tough love approach—that is, tells the parents to refuse to continue being enablers for the teenager's behavior and set standards that he must meet—the parents probably will not follow through adequately because of the cultural tendency to care for family members at a surface level.

Another example of the importance of avoiding family shame was presented by Carol Cole (1993). In her role as an emergency response worker with a county mental health unit, she received a call from neighbors, who complained of an awful stench coming from a house next door. When she arrived, she found a 40-year-old Asian American woman who was completely psychotic. She was delusional, disheveled, and disoriented, had no food in the house, and showed no signs of reality orientation. Her Asian family had immigrated to the United States 5 years earlier, and the parents had kept this 40-year-old daughter in the home with no treatment because acknowledging that a child was mentally ill would bring shame on the family. Two weeks earlier, the parents had been in a car wreck, and no one was at home to take care of the daughter. In this case, although the client was hospitalized involuntarily, the action was reframed as an opportunity to help stabilize the daughter and teach the family about available resources—in this case, resources in the Vietnamese community.

Strict approaches that require setting firm limits, such as making a child sleep outside or go to school in dirty clothes, bring shame to the whole family;

therefore, parents tend to enable irresponsible behaviors to avoid shame. To confront a child about how her or his behavior makes the family feel would be shameful, so parents' true feelings are often hidden. The child usually knows this, can take advantage of it, and can abuse the parents' acts of kindness. This situation is especially damaging when a child is addicted to drugs. Teenagers know that their parents will bail them out of jail if they are arrested or will always allow them to stay at home. Not to do so would bring shame to the family. Unfortunately, many parents of drug-addicted Asian American teenagers believe they are helping their children by taking care of their basic needs and buying them material things. This, however, reinforces the addicts' behaviors and enables further drug use. The crisis counselor must be sensitive to these cultural norms and slowly encourage open communication between generations rather than force them to take such actions as tough love.

Communication Process in Asian American Culture

Another area in which sensitivity is needed is communication style. Asian Americans have been conditioned to avoid eye contact and direct confrontations, especially with doctors and authority figures. This trait may create complications during an interview if the counselor is not aware of this cultural style. Whereas mainstream Americans may consider avoiding eye contact to be rude, Asians may feel that looking someone in the eye is rude. Also, Asian clients may feel that they cannot disagree with the counselor because of respect for the authority position. The counselor may have to encourage disagreement and define it as part of the interview process at times.

Also, if a crisis worker is working with a family, the tendency to ask family members to confront each other directly may be culturally insensitive. They will probably do best with more educational, problem-solving approaches that focus on a presenting problem. Reframing the solution as strengthening the family unit will probably be well received by Asian American clients. The crisis worker needs to be aware of the hierarchy in the family and include the most powerful family members in making decisions.

> **Example:** A 19-year-old Asian American youth was depressed about having received a C in a chemistry course. He felt ashamed and was sure his father would be angry with him for bringing disgrace on the family. He believed that his only solution was to kill himself by jumping off a tall building.

Instead of working only with this client, the counselor would be well advised to bring in the young man's parents. The client needs to be told that his suicide might bring more shame to the family than getting a C in chemistry. The worker can reframe the problem by pointing out that the lower grade in chemistry could be balanced by a high grade in another class. By asking his parents for their opinions and possible solutions, the client will feel more secure in the fact that he will not bring shame to them. Instead, the family may be brought closer together. The counselor should emphasize to the parents that their son cares so much about the family name that he was willing to sacrifice his own life for the family honor—another reframing of the situation.

TABLE 4.3 | SUMMARIZATION OF SPECIAL
CONSIDERATIONS IN WORKING WITH
MEXICAN AMERICANS, AFRICAN
AMERICANS, AND ASIAN AMERICANS

Mexican Americans
- Enmeshed family structure
- Language barriers
- Different levels of acculturation
- Strong Catholic religious focus

African Americans
- History of racism dating back to era of slavery
- Group with the most salient differences from the mainstream group
- Distrust of mainstream institutions
- Clergy serve as traditional support system when crises arise

Asian Americans
- Shame and obligation
- Rigid family roles and structures
- Counseling should be problem focused and formal

Table 4.3 summarizes salient issues for the crisis worker to remember when working with the three ethnic groups just discussed. The worker should remember, however, that each person is unique and that these issues may not apply to everyone. Most importantly, the worker must remember to understand the crisis experience from the client's point of view. Other issues may be important.

PEOPLE WITH DISABILITIES AND CRISIS INTERVENTION

(THIS SECTION WAS WRITTEN PREDOMINANTLY BY JOHN DOYLE, PhD)

When compared with the general population, persons with disabilities are more prone to crises, and as such deserve particular attention from a crisis intervention perspective.

Example: Jack, a disabled police officer in his mid-30s, has been forced to resign his position because of a diagnosis of bipolar affective disorder. Like many with this condition, even when he takes his medications as prescribed, it is difficult for him to maintain his emotional equilibrium, to the point where he requires psychiatric hospitalization about twice a year. He is also alcohol dependent, which he controls by rigorous participation in the Alcoholics Anonymous 12-step program. With the benefit of vocational rehabilitation services, Jack has been relatively successful in maintaining part-time employment.

Example: Victor, a retired teacher in his mid-60s, has been enjoying his leisure years in a wide array of activities, including travel. Suddenly and unexpectedly, his vision has deteriorated; the cause is an eye condition that is progressive and irreversible. He is no longer allowed to drive, which is a severe blow to his sense of independence. But for both him and his family, the psychological impact of his disability has proved to be the more difficult adjustment.

Example: Debbie, age 39, has a diagnosis of mild to moderate cerebral palsy and is profoundly deaf. She has always resided with her mother, who has provided her with the necessary support to live a relatively normal and independent life. Debbie has an awkward gait, which gives the impression that she is intoxicated. This appearance has led to frequent arrests by the police as she walks to and from her place of part-time employment. Her hearing impairment limits her communication skills, further complicating her ability to communicate with the police and others. Her mother, now elderly and in deteriorating health, has been Debbie's lifetime advocate and care provider.

Responses to People with Disabilities

Disability, a broad concept, is physical or mental impairment that substantially prevents or restricts the ordinary course of human development and accomplishments. Disabilities are often present from birth but can develop at any time in the life cycle. They include such clearly recognizable conditions as blindness, deafness, mental retardation, and mental illness, but also conditions that are less obvious, such as learning disabilities, AIDS, heart disease, and cancer. Depending on the severity of the impairment, the functional level of the person is impaired to a lesser or greater degree. Some people have more than one disability or struggle with both physical and mental impairments. The level of impairment dictates the degree of support needed; not only is the disabled person challenged but so are his or her family members, caregivers, and society at large.

Throughout human history, society has frequently greeted disabled people with stigma, prejudice, mistreatment, discrimination, social isolation, inferior status, and inferior services. Changing the culture of disability is an ongoing challenge. Until relatively recent times, mentally retarded people were officially referred to as idiots, feeble-minded people, imbeciles, or morons. These terms, now obsolete in professional and clinical settings, survive in everyday language as powerful derogatory epithets. It is often easier to find agreement on terms that should not be used than on terms that are suitable to use. The term *mentally retarded* has negative connotations and is being replaced in some settings by the term *developmentally disabled* or *mentally challenged*. However, the terms *disability* and *disabled* are often seen to connote weakness, dependence, abnormality, and inferiority.

Even when people have the best of intentions, they often view persons with disabilities unrealistically. Disabled people may view themselves unrealistically. On the one hand, the disability can be overestimated to a point where the individual is sentimentalized and unnecessarily relegated to a position of overdependence. On the other hand, the disability can be underestimated to the point where the person and his or her family experience endless failure and emotional frustration. Achieving a realistic balance in which the functional strengths of the individual define him or her rather than the disability can be difficult; however, achieving that balance is important in preventing crises.

The Disabled Population and the ADA

Depending on the definition applied, the number of disabled individuals in American society varies. The legal journey defining persons with disabilities and articulating their rights reached a high point when Congress passed the **Americans with Disabilities Act (ADA) of 1990,** which broadly challenges discrimination against disabled people. The ADA went into effect in July 1992. It defines a person with a disability as having a physical or mental impairment that substantially limits one or more major life activities; has a record of such an impairment; or is regarded as having such an impairment. The intent of the legislation is to make society more accessible to people with disabilities, but its implementation continues to be a major challenge. According to Census 2000, 48.9 people who were 5 years old and over living in housing units had a disability, or 19.2% of the disabled population in the United States (Stern, 2001). Congress recognizes the historical and present tendency of society to discriminate against disabled people, and mandates remedies in such areas as employment, housing, public accommodations, education, transportation, communication, recreation, institutionalization, health services, voting rights, and access to public services. It also prohibits coercion of or retaliation against people with disabilities or those who advocate for rights for the disabled.

Not only are people with disabilities discriminated against, but they are frequently abused. Women with disabilities are more likely to experience abuse by a greater number of perpetrators and for longer periods than nondisabled women (Young et al., 1997). Unfortunately, many people with disabling conditions are especially vulnerable to victimization because of their real or perceived inability to fight or flee, notify others, or testify in court. Despite the advocacy of ADA workers, crime victims with disabilities are less likely than those without disabilities to reap the benefits of the criminal justice system. The reason is that crimes against disabled victims go unreported because of victims' mobility or communication barriers, social or physical isolation, or normal feelings of shame and self-blame, or because the perpetrator of the crime is the victim's caretaker (U.S. Department of Justice, 2001).

Once the ADA was passed, one could say that people with disabilities entered mainstream society. However, their challenges continue. The main controversy concerns the cost of changes for accommodating disabled people in both the public and private sectors of society. According to Title II of the ADA, discrimination of any kind on the basis of disability is prohibited. Community agencies, including the police force, firefighting force, state legislature, city councils, state courts, public schools, public recreation departments, and departments of motor vehicle licensing, must allow people with disabilities to participate fully in all of their services, programs, and activities. An example of the effect of the ADA on the police force can be seen in the **Police Executive Research Forum,** which provides a detailed training curriculum and model policy for responding to people with mental illness, developmental disabilities, and speech and hearing impairments.

Vulnerable Subgroups within the Disabled Population

Because the ADA has been passed, many people with disabilities can now live more as part of mainstream society. For instance, wheelchair-accessible buildings allow many with physical disabilities to enjoy social and vocational independence. However, some subgroups within the disabled population are particularly prone to crises, and there is no simple way to offset their vulnerability. The most vulnerable groups are fragile elderly people, mentally ill people, and developmentally disabled people.

Disabled Elderly People Elderly people are not automatically disabled. However, there is a greater risk of disability as a person ages. In 1994 and 1995, 52.5% of people over 65 years of age reported having at least one disability, and 33% reported having at least one severe disability. Over 6 million, or 21%, had difficulty in carrying out activities of daily living. As people grow older, there is a corresponding increase in disabilities. Walker (1994) argues that prevention of disabilities in older adults is a shared responsibility, involving the elderly individual, healthcare providers, and society at large. Individual choice is not sufficient; rather, there is a need for a broad social commitment to the promotion of health. However, diseases are significant risk factors for disability in elderly people, and age itself is a risk factor for those over 85 years of age. Hogan, Ebly, and Fung (1999) examined cognitively intact community resident seniors and found that age alone accounts for the fact that twice as many in the 85-plus age group are physically disabled compared with the 65- to 84-year-old age group. Hence, disease prevention will not necessarily impede disability in older seniors. Compared with the 65- to 80-year-old population, those over 80 are twice as likely to have difficulty with such activities as bathing, dressing, eating, preparing meals, shopping, managing money, and taking medication.

It is clear from the literature that intervention for elderly people with disabilities must be holistic in nature, involving a network of community resources. In a study of the characteristics of older adults with intellectual disabilities who required crisis intervention, Davidson and colleagues (1995) concluded that intellectually disabled adults require comprehensive age-span community mental health and behavioral supports. The severity of the behavioral crises decreases over the life cycle, but the need for intervention remains constant. The need for intervention is not limited to elderly persons with a disability. Altman, Cooper, and Cunningham (1999) described the struggles of a family with a disabled elder. Families experience an increased number of emotional, financial, and health crises. Alzheimer's dementia and senile dementia are particularly stressful for the family. Graham (1989) points out that as these diseases and disabilities progress, day-care placement may be necessary; even with day care, the stress level does not necessarily decrease for family caregivers. Frail elderly people are the most vulnerable to neglect and abuse by caregivers, both professionals and family members.

Talecxih (2001) reports that by 2050 the number of elderly people requiring institutional care will likely more than double, from 5 million to 11 million. The elderly population will be more diverse, so the long-term care workforce will have to be more culturally competent. Human service workers generally will need more training in dealing with the problems of an aging population (Rosen & Zlotnik, 2001).

Mentally Disabled People Although it is more difficult to define and measure mental disabilities, the debilitating nature of emotional and psychological problems is quite clear. Under the ADA, a mental impairment includes any "mental or psychological disorder, such as . . . emotional or mental illness." Among the examples cited are "major depression, bipolar disorder, anxiety disorders (which include panic disorder, obsessive disorder, and PTSD), schizophrenia, and personality disorders." Comer (1995) gives the following statistics on mental illness in the United States: 13% have significant anxiety disorders; 6% have serious depression; 5% have debilitating personality disorders; 1% has schizophrenia; 1% has Alzheimer's disease; and 10% are suffering from drug and alcohol difficulties.

With the introduction of the major tranquilizer medications in the 1950s, psychotic behaviors could be controlled, and the treatment of people with serious mental illnesses changed significantly. Before this new treatment mode, those with serious mental illness were confined to psychiatric hospitals, which were locked facilities. The major tranquilizers made deinstitutionalization possible. Treatment is now community based; and hospitalizations, especially long-term stays, are avoided as much as possible. Further goals of deinstitutionalization are the promotion of the rights and independence of mentally ill people and a more cost-effective delivery of services. The **National Institute of Mental Health** indicates that the number of institutionalized mental health patients decreased from a high of 559,000 in 1955 to 69,000 in 1995.

The **Community Mental Health Act of 1963** set goals for the provision of community-based services for the mentally disabled. These services include inpatient care for seriously ill patients, with the goal of returning them to the community as soon as possible; outpatient clinics for ongoing care; partial hospitalization, where patients can go home at night and on weekends; 24-hour crisis centers; and consultation, education, and information services for those who regularly interact with these disabled people in the community. Unfortunately, the provision of these community-based services has lagged, making deinstitutionalization, at best, a measured success. Although the major tranquilizers work well for seriously mentally ill people when they are in the hospital setting and help them return to the community, individuals who do not have the support of friends, are unemployed, or do not have access to ongoing mental health services are destined for failure in community-based living. Some observers feel that the deinstitutionalization policy for the mentally ill has been a dismal failure. Others see it as a success in that it promotes civil liberties for those with serious mental illness. Johnson (1990) points out that with certain supports in place, such as housing, outreach by human service workers, independent living skills support, and occasional hospitalizations for stabilization of their condition, community-based placement is appropriate. Without the necessary supports, seriously mentally ill people in the community are in a permanent state of crisis. Unfortunately, people in the community often see these people as a public nuisance that should be controlled by the criminal justice system; this is an inappropriate and highly unfair assessment.

It can be argued that institutionalization in the absence of proper community support is more humane for seriously mentally ill people because they do not fall victim to homelessness, hunger, abuse, or the criminal justice system and because, with their limited coping skills, they avoid living in a permanent state of crisis. It is also clear that because of the number of community support services needed to help some of these people, community placement is not necessarily less costly than institutionalization.

Developmentally Disabled People   The developmentally disabled population includes those with mental retardation, cerebral palsy, epilepsy, autism, and other neurological disorders. In particular, mentally retarded people have been unnecessarily institutionalized and subject to involuntary sterilization. The deinstitutionalization movement of the 1970s reflected a concern for the civil rights of the developmentally disabled; today, very few are institutionalized. The guiding principle is that they have the right to develop as fully as they can and live as normally and independently as possible. Most now live more independently with their families or in group homes. The movement of developmentally disabled people into the community means that crises that once occurred behind the walls of state institutions now are seen in every community. There is an ongoing need to meet this inevitable problem. Community-based living places more demands on the limited coping skills of the developmentally disabled, making them even more prone to crises.

Shoham-Vardi and his colleagues (1996, p. 109) report that up to 60% of persons with developmental disabilities have behavioral and psychiatric disorders; the recidivism rate is 88% in 2 years. As reported by these authors, for developmentally disabled persons under age 30 years, the strongest predictors of recidivism are living apart from the family and an initial diagnosis of self-injurious behavior; for those over age 30 years, a history of aggression is the strongest predictor of recidivism. This population places special demands on the community with regard to creating and maintaining appropriate resources to meet their complex needs.

Like the mentally ill population, newly independent developmentally disabled people can fall victim—some say unfairly—to the criminal justice system. For example, a 23-year-old person with mental retardation from Tulare, California, is serving a third-strike prison sentence of 28 years to life for stealing a VCR and some jewelry from a residence. His previous "strikes" were for arson: The first time, he set fire to a trash can, and the second time, a fire began in a truck where it appeared he had been playing with matches. It could be argued that under the old system, this individual would have resided in the protective environment of a state institution and would not have become involved in the state criminal justice system. Others argue that there is a price for independence that cannot be measured by the mistakes of a few.

Like the general population generally, more developmentally disabled people are living to be elderly. Advances in medicine have helped these people, just as they have helped nondisabled people. The longer life span means that developmentally disabled people need more extensive and complex interventions over the life cycle. For the first time in history, these people are outliving their parents (Ansello, 1988). Estimates of the number of elderly developmentally disabled people vary from at least 4 in every 1,000 older persons (Janicki, 1991) to as many as 1 in every 100 older persons (Ansello & Eustis, 1992). To prevent or delay institutionalization, strengthen independence, and enhance daily functioning of the older population with developmental disabilities, a new emphasis on service needs must emerge. Collaboration is critical between service providers and family caregivers in serving the needs of the developmentally disabled elderly.

Coogle and his colleagues (1995) argue for resource sharing and collaboration among the developmentally disabled providers and other human service networks, and also for a managed approach to intervention in order to avoid costly duplication of services. They further argue for education of the public and community leaders about those with lifelong disabilities and their families; increased funding for supportive housing and independent living centers; advocacy for older adults with developmental disabilities and their families so they can secure community-based long-term care; respite care and income support; and an increase in federal and state resources for continued community living. Zola (1988) believes that the aged and disabled populations should be served together because of their similar conditions, the technical and medical requirements of their care, and the full implications of the home care revolution. The traditional approach of dividing them into two opposing entities is a form of unnecessary segregation.

Crisis Intervention Strategies for Persons with Disabilities

Effective intervention for people with disabilities requires detailed knowledge of this population, information on their civil and legal rights, a willingness to advocate for those rights, and comprehensive knowledge of available sources of support and intervention.

Crises do not occur in a vacuum. For disabled people, crises often occur because helpers do not have adequate knowledge and understanding of a particular disability and fail to establish the necessary support systems. For instance, a high-functioning autistic person who works in a predictable environment with structured supervision can be extremely productive and successful. However, because such an individual typically has great difficulty with social and environmental transitions, any change in work routine or personnel can provoke a major crisis. To decrease the likelihood of such a crisis requires not only the maintenance of a predictable work routine but ongoing education for other employees and the management staff on how to successfully interact with this individual. This requires a considerable commitment on the part of all concerned. Depending on the disability and circumstances, similar preventive strategies need to be employed.

Case management is one of the most important developments in human services in the past half century. Schneider (1988) emphasizes the importance of case management as an intervention strategy. It is consumer centered; embraces the elements of screening, assessment, specific goals, interdisciplinary and interagency cooperation, and measurable outcomes; and is subject to monitoring and evaluation. Case management is a proactive, positive way of intervening with regularity with the chronically disabled, a way of anticipating situations before they become full-blown crises.

Effective crisis intervention and prevention are rooted in a system of comprehensive collaboration. Knowledge of available services and the ways in which they can be accessed is essential. For example, the 1975 federal **Education for All Handicapped Children Act** (Public Law 94-142), updated in 1997 as the **Individuals with Disabilities Education Act (IDEA)**, is just one of many federal programs for the disabled. It mandates free, appropriate, individualized public education for handicapped children—those with learning handicaps, developmental disabilities, orthopedic conditions, and mental illness. Local school districts play a major role in the lives of disabled children from the time they are 3 years of age until they reach 22 years of age, so an important intervention is assisting the disabled and their families in using this resource.

People who are not disabled, even human service workers, react differently to disabled people. Some common reactions are fear, repulsion, anxiety about loss and dependence, embarrassment, and avoidance of social contact. Working with disabled people may be perceived as less prestigious than working with other types of people. Legislation mandating full inclusion of the disabled population is one thing; implementation of the legislation is another. Both physical and psychological obstacles to inclusion remain, including the cost of services, competing interests, and discrimination, as well as the self-limiting roles of disabled people themselves. This population requires meaningful intervention and attention, not stigmatization or sentimentalization.

THE SUBCULTURE OF GAYS, LESBIANS, BISEXUALS, AND TRANSGENDERS

Terms that are commonly used in discussions of the gay, lesbian, bisexual, and transgender population are listed below. These individuals are sometimes referred to as the g/l/b/t population. The definitions may be helpful to the reader.

bisexual: A person who experiences social and romantic attraction to both genders.

closet gay: A person who is unaware of his or her homosexuality or is unwilling to publicly acknowledge it; such a person may be described as "being in the closet."

coming out: The process of identifying and coming to terms with one's homosexuality. The term is also used to describe a homosexual person who is telling another person that he or she is gay.

gay: A man that is mostly sexually attracted to men.

heterosexism: The attitude of overt or covert bias against homosexuals based on the belief that heterosexuality is superior.

homophobia: Unreasonable fear or hatred of a homosexual.

homosexuality: Sexual desires primarily for a person of the same sex.

lesbian: A woman who feels sexual desire predominantly for other women.

transgender: A person who has experienced himself or herself socially, emotionally, and psychologically as male if the person was born female, or female if the person was born male.

There seems to be a trend among adults toward more acceptance of gays and lesbians in society (Yang, 1999). This is evident in the ratings of television shows that have been nominated for and won Emmy awards, such as *Queer Eye for the Straight Guy* and *Will and Grace*, and in the open disclosure by some celebrities of their homosexual identity. However, many people still have negative feelings toward individuals who live openly gay and lesbian lifestyles. Adults who present themselves to the world as gay make themselves open to criticism and rejection by family, friends, and co-workers. Recent political discussions have highlighted the ongoing debate about whether gays should be allowed to be legally married with the same rights as heterosexual married couples. Proponents of gay marriage believe that not allowing gay marriage is a form of discrimination. This is such an important issue that it has become a platform upon which certain major political parties run.

Keeping one's homosexuality hidden can lead to mental health problems such as anxiety and depression. The closet gay must always worry about keeping his or her true sexual orientation concealed. Often these people must lie to those they care about, and this duplicity leads to negative feelings.

Crisis hot lines and centers have been established to help this population live healthy gay and lesbian lifestyles, disclose their orientation to others, and learn how to handle rejection from society. A counselor must be sensitive to the special issues faced by both the closet gay and the openly gay person. It is best to find out how each individual perceives his or her situation and continue with the interview following the ABC model. Knowing about community resources is a big help.

Typical Issues Facing G/L/B/T Persons in Crisis

Unlike other minority groups, when an individual accepts the fact that he or she is gay, lesbian, bisexual, or transgender, he or she usually feels isolated from family and friends. Many times the child grows up in a home where he or she receives messages full of heterosexism (i.e., that the only proper sexual relations are between females and males) and homophobia (i.e., the fear of homosexuality). When individuals begin to recognize themselves as being gay or lesbian, they must also contend with their own homophobia. They often prefer to deny the possibility of being gay or lesbian.

Families of these individuals also experience crises. Parents are not prepared to raise or be involved in the life of a gay child. They often feel like failures and feel guilty about their resentment of their child's sexual orientation. Many parents believe that being gay is an illness and seek treatment for their child's homosexuality, despite the fact that, since 1974, psychiatrists have not considered homosexuality to be a mental disorder.

Suicide is a big risk for individuals in the beginning stages of discovering their gay sexual orientation as well as for gay persons who experience societal discrimination. The news media often has reports of hate crimes against gays. Gay persons have been socialized in a culture that fears homosexuality on moral grounds. Judeo-Christian culture has emphasized that sodomy is a sin. Therefore, gay individuals often experience self-loathing for a time until they can come to terms with the reality of their sexuality.

Although certain sexual acts, such as sodomy and oral sex, are illegal in some states, being gay is not illegal. In fact, being gay is much more than a sexual act. People who are gay build lives together, build friendship networks, work in many fields, and live productive lives.

Coming Out

Coming out does not happen overnight; it is a process that happens over time. The phrase usually refers to telling someone of one's gay sexual orientation. It is often done in stages rather than as a single event. This process of accepting one's gay sexuality usually begins deep within a person's psyche as he or she experiences feelings, thoughts, and desires related to his or her sexuality. There may be an inner battle as the person fights with cultural homophobic norms. When an individual is socialized to believe that gays are deviants, it is difficult to come to terms with one's own feelings of homosexuality without believing that one is deviant.

The person coming out often contends with shame that he or she imposes on himself or herself or that society imposes on him or her. Fear is a big factor as well. Some of this fear is realistic, as rejection from family and friends is a common consequence of coming out. Each time an individual informs someone that he is gay, he must face the fear of the unknown. Because of societal discrimination, the person may fear losing a job, losing a home (or not being allowed to purchase a home), or losing respect from others. The decision to come out, then, must not be an impulsive act but rather one that is well thought out and strategic. A crisis counselor can assist persons as they move slowly through this process to help reduce negative consequences.

Once there is an internal acceptance of being homosexual, individuals begin the process of reprogramming their ideas about being gay and turn the shame into pride. There may be a phase of experimentation with their new identity when they tell friends and family or connect with the gay community through nightclubs and community centers.

The age of an individual who is coming out makes a difference in the consequences in his or her life. For example, a middle-aged woman who had been married for 15 years and has children will need to think carefully before coming out. It could take several years for her to make the decision to live as a lesbian, even though she clearly experiences her sexuality that way. She must proceed slowly and deal with all the members of her family so as to decrease trauma for everyone. The crisis worker should not encourage people to come out immediately but rather guide clients into their own coming-out process. The counselor may even play devil's advocate and help clients question whether the gay feelings are real. This does not mean that the counselor discourages a person from being gay. It is not a disorder that needs to be fixed but, rather, an identity with social consequences. This fact must be part of crisis intervention.

A 25-year-old woman who lives on her own, has good self-esteem, and can rely on a good support system might have an easier time coming out. However, keep in mind that coming out is probably never easy because of societal taboos, parental reactions, and reactions of friends and co-workers who did not know about the person's gay sexuality. Some people believe that being gay is fine until one of their own loved ones comes out as gay. Family members might go into a state of shock when they find out that a child is gay.

> **Example:** A 17-year-old girl had been struggling with her sexuality for 2 years. She had engaged in moderate lesbian sexual activities with a girl on her basketball team. She kept the truth about this relationship from her parents and said the other girl was just a good friend. The girl finally told her mother that she was bisexual and wanted to date males and females. The mother became hysterical and said that the girl was just confused and would eventually realize she was totally straight. Soon, the girl met another female who was a lesbian. The girl became very involved with her and realized that she was a lesbian herself, not bisexual. She told her mother, who went into shock. All the mother's hopes and dreams about having a big wedding for her daughter and future son-in-law and having grandchildren were lost. The mother could not see that there could still be a future with her daughter. The father disowned the daughter.

During the coming-out process, there is an increased risk of suicidal thinking and attempts. The individual may feel hopeless about the future, helpless, and worthless, and may experience many painful feelings. Add to these feelings increased social isolation, and the risk of suicide can be quite high. The crisis worker should evaluate suicide regularly when a client is experiencing this type of crisis, particularly when disclosures are being made and rejection by loved ones is possible.

Remember that there will be consequences when a person comes out. The counselor must not make the decision about when to come out for a client. Instead, the crisis worker should help client make his or her own decision by using empowering and support statements. By discussing the consequences of not coming out, such as emotional repression, unhappiness in relationships, and pervasive guilt and shame, persons considering coming out might be helped to see that the immediate consequences of possible rejection are better than a life of permanent dissatisfaction.

The crisis counselor can say that although friends and family may be rejecting at first, attitudes change over time. Just as clients may not have been able to accept their gay sexuality at first, loved ones may not be accepting, either. Time is an important factor. Support groups are useful. The crisis worker should refer clients to a group in which others can relate to the dilemma first-hand. Being reassured by educational statements that homosexuality is not a disease can often help the client feel better as well. Many communities have gay/lesbian/bisexual/transgender centers that provide services for the many issues facing the gay population. Most colleges have special centers for gay people. Even some high schools have gay and lesbian associations. Crisis workers may also provide family counseling to mediate between children and parents or between spouses. Of course, suicide assessment should be done when clients are depressed.

Transgender people are usually men. They have experienced themselves emotionally, psychologically, and socially as females since childhood, despite having a male body. As an adult, a transgender may choose to change his physiology by taking female hormones to enlarge his breasts or by undergoing major reconstructive surgery to create a completely female body. He may then choose to identify himself as a "she" in society and even on legal documents. The process of becoming a transgender may take years. Many "sex-change" surgeons require that patients receive psychological assessment prior to this dramatic life change. Some transgenders do not undergo full sex-change surgery, as it is expensive. Instead, they live as women by dressing and grooming themselves as women and by taking hormones. Because this procedure is not common, most people in society have had little contact with transgenders. Most stereotypes about transgenders probably have to do with them being gay "drag queens" or "freaks." Human service workers will find transgenders to be fairly normal except that they are not happy living as the biological gender with which they were born. Some may be gay (attracted to men after sex-change surgery), and others may be attracted to women.

Case Vignettes

The following case vignettes may be useful to practice once you have studied the ABC model presented in the next chapter. Come back to these cases when you are ready to practice role-playing.

Case 1   A Mexican American woman comes to see you because she has been depressed since her last child entered kindergarten. She does not sleep well, is nervous, and fights to get her child to obey her.

What cultural issues are at stake here? How would you proceed?

Hint: Offer psychoeducational information regarding child development.

Hint: Offer supportive statements about letting go of her child.

Hint: Reframe the child's rebelliousness as a sign that the mother has raised a secure child who can function in school.

Hint: Empower the mother by pointing out how her role as a mother has just changed, not been eliminated. She has new tasks to master now, which will be even more challenging than when her child was younger.

Hint: Offer educational information about the possibility of different rates of acculturation as a child enters school.

Case 2 A 19-year-old Vietnamese female college student is distressed because she has fallen in love with an American boy. She wants to spend time with him, but her parents expect her to stay at home when she is not at school. She wants to kill herself because she is so depressed.

How can you help her? What must you keep in mind?

Hint: Offer supportive statements about how difficult it is to respect one's parents and still have one's own life.

Hint: Educate her about the different rates of acculturation of her and her parents.

Hint: Empower her by focusing on what she can do to feel better; talk about ways that she can show respect to her parents and perhaps still see the boy at school.

Hint: Conduct a suicide assessment and discuss the fact that if she killed herself, she would bring more shame on her family than she would by dating a boy.

Hint: Offer to speak with her parents about the situation and let them know how much their daughter respects them—so much that she would rather kill herself than shame them. They would not want her to kill herself over this situation.

Case 3 A 14-year-old African American boy is sent for counseling by his school counselor because he has not been coming to school and is not performing when he is in school. His mother brings him to the appointment. She is in a hurry because she is on her lunch break from her full-time job. His father does not live with them, though he comes around frequently.

Who might be available for support? What biases must you avoid?

Hint: Find out who the teen and his mother live with, and if is there a grandmother available to help out.

Hint: Educate the boy about the need to finish high school and the special importance of this for African Americans because discrimination is bad enough, even when one has a diploma.

Hint: Encourage the father to be involved in the situation and be a good role model.

Hint: Empathize with the teen about the fact that school is not always easy or fun.

Hint: Assess the teen's level of depression and ask about what has been happening in his life recently.

Case 4 A man is in a wheelchair because his legs were paralyzed in a surf-board accident a year ago. He comes to you because he is lonely. Last weekend at a party he talked with a woman that he had met once before, prior to his accident. He wants to date her but is afraid she will not want to date him because of his disability.

Hint: Offer support statements about how difficult it is to be disabled and have to change one's lifestyle.

Hint: Empower him by helping him focus on what he can do. Maybe this girl will not be his lover, but she may want to hang out with him.

Hint: Reframe the situation as a chance to find out how females will react to his advances. Because he had met the woman before, she may be willing to be honest with him. He needs to find out how women feel about a man in a wheelchair.

Hint: Educate him about the fact that many men in wheelchairs are married and that people can be sexual without having sexual intercourse.

Case 5   A 17-year-old girl comes in because she is depressed and her mother is worried about her. The girl has begun a sexual relationship with a female basketball teammate, but claims that she still likes boys. The mother insists that her daughter is not a lesbian. The father will not have anything to do with his daughter if she chooses to date girls.

Hint: Empathize with all about how difficult it is to deal with sexuality issues.

Hint: Educate about the fact that a 17-year-old has not completely formed her identity.

Hint: Educate about homosexuality, bisexuality, and heterosexuality (you may need to read up on these subjects).

Hint: Focus on the cognitions underlying the mother's distress and the father's rejection.

Hint: Talk with the daughter alone about the coming-out process.

KEY TERMS FOR STUDY

African Americans: As seen by the crisis worker, a minority group that does not use the mental health system often. The historical roots of this group help explain why its members tend to resolve crises through the extended family and clergy rather than through governmental or other mainstream agencies. Racism and discrimination are still common problems for this group and must be kept in mind by crisis workers. Religion has historically been important in helping this group to get through the many daily stressors they encounter in America.

Alzheimer's dementia: A progressive disease that usually begins in elderly people. There is deterioration of mental functioning, particularly short-term memory. When the brain loses its ability to maintain regulatory functions such as breathing and eating, the person may die.

American with Disabilities Act of 1990: The intent of this legislation is to make society more accessible to people with disabilities. It defines disabilities and challenges the discrimination associated with disabilities.

Asian Americans: As seen by the crisis worker, a minority group whose members may seek the services of mental health workers in crises, but who prefer a problem-solving approach similar to that used by a family doctor to treat physical illnesses. The crisis worker must be aware of issues of shame and obligation because they may come into play when a family member is in crisis. Crisis workers must also respect the family structure to prevent resistance to proposed coping alternatives.

case management: An effective approach to working with individuals and families in which a disability is a factor. It includes such elements as screening, assessment, setting goals, interagency and interdisciplinary cooperation, and measurable outcomes. It is a proactive way to regularly intervene with the high-risk disabled population in order to prevent full-blown crises.

development of cultural sensitivity: A four-stage process during which counselors learn to consider cultural factors when they are conducting counseling sessions. The stages are (1) lack of awareness of cultural issues; (2) heightened awareness of culture; (3) realization of the burden of considering culture; and (4) beginnings of cultural sensitivity.

developmental disabilities: Neurological disorders such as mental retardation, cerebral palsy, epilepsy, and autism.

disability: Physical or mental impairment that substantially prevents or restricts the ordinary course of human development and accomplishments.

mainstreamed: People with disabilities who function in society with as much independence as possible both socially and vocationally.

Mexican Americans: As seen by the crisis worker, a cultural group whose members seek mental health services more often than African Americans or Asian Americans. Mexican Americans suffer crises related to language barriers, religious differences, and cultural differences in child rearing. Families tend to be enmeshed, and children are encouraged to be dependent.

role of systems theory: An important element in working with clients from minority groups. The crisis worker must identify family roles and allowable behavior for a particular cultural group; these may be different from mainstream roles and behaviors. Imposing mainstream psychological theories on other cultures is often counterproductive.

senile dementia: Deterioration in mental faculties found in some elderly people. It might include poor memory, delusions, confabulations (making up memories to fill in gaps), and socially inappropriate behaviors.

THE ABC MODEL OF CRISIS INTERVENTION

The ABC model of crisis intervention is a method for conducting very brief mental health interviews with clients whose functioning level has decreased following a psychosocial stressor. This model follows the formula presented in Chapter 1 regarding the process of crisis formation. It is a problem-focused approach and is most effectively applied within 4 to 6 weeks of the stressor. Identifying the cognitions of the client as they relate to the precipitating event and then altering them to help decrease unmanageable feelings is the central focus of the method. In addition, providing community referrals and other resources such as reading material is also essential in applying this model.

Caplan and Lindemann first conceptualized the crisis intervention approach in the 1940s (Caplan, 1964; Lindemann, 1944); others have since developed models that use the principles and techniques of these founders. The ABC model of crisis intervention presented in this text has its origins in a variety of sources. It is loosely based on Jones's (1968) A-B-C method of crisis management, with its three-stage process: A, achieving contact; B, boiling the problem down to basics; and C, coping. Moline (1986), a former professor at California State University, Fullerton, developed a course called Crisis Intervention, in which she used a modified version of Jones's model. From her lecture notes and from discussions with her about how she organized the course, the author developed, as noted in Chapter 2, the ABC model of crisis intervention discussed in this book. Over a period of 20 years, the author has expanded and revised the ABC model. Revisions are based on current information from experts in the community who provide crisis intervention for a variety of populations, the author's experiences in teaching the model to students and community counselors and receiving feedback from these students, and the author's experiences as a counselor in public, private, and nonprofit agency settings.

Other models have also influenced the ABC model of crisis intervention in terms of the particular structure and stages. Structuring the counseling process around certain phases or stages is not a new phenomenon. It has been done by mental health practitioners since the days of such founding theorists as Sullivan (1954) and Adler (Corey, 1996, p. 143). The phases are not linear but, like those of the ABC model, are best "understood as a weaving that leads to a tapestry" (Corey, 1996, p. 143). Adler developed a four-phase model for the therapeutic process: phase 1, establishing the relationship; phase 2, exploring the individual's dynamics; phase 3, encouraging insight; and phase 4, helping with reorientation (Corey, 1996, pp. 143–150). These four phases are similar to those of the ABC model:

A: Developing and maintaining contact (corresponds with Adler's phase 1)
B: Identifying the problem and providing therapeutic interaction (corresponds with Adler's phase 2 and phase 3)
C: Coping (corresponds with Adler's phase 4)

Sullivan (1954) also used a phase model to structure psychiatric interviews. His stages can be seen to correspond with the stages of the ABC model: phase 1, the formal inception (analogous to A of the ABC model); phase 2, the reconnaissance, and phase 3, the detailed inquiry (analogous to B); and phase 4, termination (analogous to C).

Although the ABC model of crisis intervention has a three-stage approach, in an actual interview the components of any one stage could be used at any time. Readers should keep this thought in mind during the discussion of each stage that follows. The crisis worker will learn how to integrate the stages through practice and experience.

A: DEVELOPING AND MAINTAINING RAPPORT

The foundation of crisis intervention is the development of rapport—a state of understanding and comfort—between client and counselor. As the client begins to feel rapport, trust and openness follow, allowing the interview to proceed. Before delving into the client's personal world, the counselor must achieve this personal contact. The counseling relationship is unique in this regard; before any work can be done, the client must feel understood and accepted by the counselor. A student of the author summed up this need quite appropriately: "People don't care what you know, until they know that you care."

By learning several basic attending skills, the beginning crisis counselor can develop the self-confidence needed to make contact with someone in crisis. Use of these basic rapport-building communication skills invites the client to talk, brings calm control to the situation, allows the client to talk about the facts of the situation and the counselor to hear and empathize with the client's feelings, and lets the client know that the counselor is concerned and respectful.

Remember that the interview process does not proceed in a linear fashion; the various attending skills can be interwoven as appropriate. For example, the counselor may ask a question before reflecting or may reflect before asking a question.

Unlike other approaches to counseling, crisis intervention does not typically include the use of such techniques as interpretation or direct advice giving. These techniques generally require a therapeutic relationship of long duration before they are effective; in crisis intervention, developing such a relationship is not practical. Although it may be tempting to jump in and tell clients what is wrong with them and what to do about it, the crisis interventionist is encouraged not to do this. The basic attending skills are a useful alternative to the sometimes rote practice of asking routine questions and giving routine advice and interpretations. Sometimes, clients are just not routine!

The primary purpose of using the basic attending skills is to gain a clear understanding of the internal experience of the crisis as the client sees it. Only when the counselor truly understands can he or she help to bring change to the client's subjective distress and assist the client in improving his or her functioning.

Table 5.1 can be used as a guide for the beginning counselor. It is not meant to be followed as a linear script but rather as a reminder of the skills the counselor is to use throughout the interview. Skill proficiency columns are built into the table to allow evaluation of student performance by the course instructor.

Attending Behavior

The most basic skill of helping is listening. Appropriate verbal and nonverbal behavior—that is, attending behavior—is the hallmark of a helping interview. Good eye contact, attentive body language, expressive vocal style, and verbal following are valuable listening tools, but they are not always present. The next time you carry on a conversation with a friend, observe whether these behaviors are in evidence. Using a soft, soothing voice, showing an interested face, having relaxed posture, leaning toward the client, making direct eye contact, and maintaining close physical proximity (Cormier et al., 1986, p. 30) are all ways to convey warmth and are part of active listening. These attending behaviors "demonstrate to the client that you are with him or her and indeed are listening," enabling the client to talk more freely (Ivey, Gluckstern, & Ivey, 1997, p. 19).

Active listening requires being able to observe the client and at the same time pay attention to how one should best react to the client. Try the following exercise.

Exercise

Break into groups of three or four. Using the basic attending skills evaluation sheet in Table 5.1, rate each other on attending behaviors. One person can play the client and another can be a crisis worker. A third can be the rater. If there is a fourth, that person can be an observer. The rater also enhances her or his skills of observation while giving feedback to the counselor. After this exercise, have

TABLE 5.1 | BASIC ATTENDING SKILLS

| | Skill Proficiency | | |
	Good	Fair	Poor
Attending behavior			
Eye contact			
Warmth			
Body posture			
Vocal style			
Verbal following			
Overall empathy (focus on client)			
Questioning			
Open-ended			
Close-ended			
Paraphrasing			
Restating in own words			
Clarifying			
Reflection			
Painful feelings			
Positive feelings			
Ambivalent feelings			
Nonverbal feelings			
Summarization			
Tying together precipitating event, subjective distress, and cognitive elements			

Source: From Basic Attending Skills, Third Edition, by A. E. Ivey, N. B. Gluckstern, and M. B. Ivey, pp. 19, 20–21, 35, 56, and 92. Copyright © 1997 Microtaining Associates. Reprinted with permission.

some fun exaggerating an interview in which the crisis worker does not employ these behaviors (i.e., has poor eye contact, is cold, keeps arms folded, does not pay attention verbally). This behavior will impress on everyone what not to do!

Crisis workers must remember that the attending behavior of different cultural and ethnic groups may vary in style, and these helpers may need to adapt when working with the groups discussed earlier. Ivey and colleagues (1997, pp. 20–21) have summarized typical variations:

• *Eye Contact:* African Americans, Latin Americans, and Native Americans may avoid eye contact as a sign of respect. With Latinos, direct sustained eye contact can represent a challenge to authority. A bowed head may be a sign of respect from Native Americans.

- *Body Language:* The public behavior of African Americans may seem emotionally intense and demonstrative to European Americans. A slap on the back may be insulting to an Asian American or a Latin American.
- *Vocal Style:* Latin Americans often begin meetings with lengthy greetings and pleasant talk before addressing key issues. European Americans tend to value a quiet, controlled vocal style; other groups may see this as manipulative or cold.
- *Verbal Following:* Asian Americans may prefer a more indirect and subtle communication and consider the African American or European American style too direct and confrontational. Personal questions may be especially offensive to Native Americans. (Reprinted with permission from Ivey, A. E., Gluckstern, N. B., & Ivey, M. B. *Basic Attending Skills,* 3rd ed. Pp. 19, 20–21, 35, 56, and 92. © 1997 by Microtraining Associates.)

Questioning

Asking clients pertinent questions is an invitation to them to talk. Open-ended questions provide room for clients to express their real selves without categories imposed by the interviewer. They allow clients an opportunity to explore their thoughts and feelings with the support of the interviewer. Close-ended questions can help the interviewer gather factual information such as age or marital status. However, clients frequently feel attacked or defensive with certain close-ended questions (such as "why" questions), which should be used sparingly if at all (Ivey et al., 1997, p. 35).

Beginning counseling students tend to ask "do you, have you, could you, and would you" questions. These types of close-ended questions can be answered with a "yes" or "no" by clients, with the result that an interview bogs down. Counselors should avoid these types of close-ended questions, asking more specific open-ended questions instead.

Try to tie your open-ended questions to what the client has just said. Questions that begin with "what" and "how" are very effective in allowing the client to explore his or her ideas and feelings. When the question is posed effectively, it helps move the interview along and allows gathering essential information about the nature of the crisis. Remember, it is all right to ask pointed open-ended questions when they relate to what the client has just said, and, hence, verbal following is extremely important to proper questioning. Whenever a client offers a new word or expresses energy behind what he or she says, the counselor should ask a question that helps him or her to better understand the meaning of the word or the energy. Never assume that you know what the client means. Inquire!

The following dialogue between a client and a crisis worker shows an appropriate use of questions.

> CLIENT: "I am so angry at my husband. He won't talk to me anymore and we just don't communicate at all."

CRISIS WORKER: "What do you mean by communicate?"

CLIENT: "He refuses to sit down and listen to me. I have no idea what his problem is. I can't get him to tell me anything. He obviously doesn't want to be around, but I don't know why."

CRISIS WORKER: "What makes you think he doesn't want to be around?"

CLIENT: "He is never home. He stays late at work, out with his friends every night, and is gone on the weekends. I don't know how long I can stand it."

CRISIS WORKER: "What do you mean by you don't know how long you can stand it?"

CLIENT: "Well, I am crying every night, my kids wonder where their dad is, and I am miserable and don't want to live like this."

(At this point, a reflection of feelings would be helpful, as would some close-ended questions about the kids' ages.)

Of course, these are not the only questions that could be asked. But notice that each question relates to what the client has just said, which has the effect of unrolling the client's cognitive and emotional experience. A useful metaphor is to think of the client's cognitive schema as a tree. The client presents the counselor with the trunk in the beginning. As the interview progresses, there is movement up the trunk and onto the branches. Each question allows movement onto the smaller branches and twigs, until the entire tree has been explored and is viewed in its totality. All branches, twigs, and leaves are connected to the trunk, whether directly or indirectly. When the counselor can see the tree fully, the nature of the crisis can be fully understood, and movement into offering coping strategies and altering cognitions can be accomplished.

Below are some examples of poorly worded questions and appropriately worded questions.

Poorly Worded Counselor Questions	Appropriately Worded Counselor Questions
Do you feel sad about losing your husband?	How do you feel about losing your husband?
Have you tried to talk to your father?	What have you done?
Could you tell me more about your sadness?	What is your sadness like for you?

Providing information in response to open-ended questions is generally more comfortable for clients than giving answers to 20 close-ended intake questions. There is a time and place for close-ended questions, usually when a fact is needed and during suicide assessments. Although it is true that many counselors must complete forms for their agencies, this does not mean that the interview should be a series of close-ended questions. Interweaving close-ended questions with open-ended questions, reflection, and paraphrasing should allow a counselor to complete the intake forms in most agencies. This takes practice, but clients benefit from this style.

Following are some examples of effective open-ended and close-ended questions. Included are suggestions for changing "why" questions into open-ended questions. Role-play these questions with friends.

Effective Open-Ended Questions	Appropriate Close-Ended Questions
How have you been feeling?	How long have you been married?
What is the worst part for you of being raped?	Have you been checked by a doctor yet?
What is it like for you to be diagnosed with AIDS?	Are you taking any medications?
How are you doing at work lately?	How old are your children?
What are your thoughts about death?	Has your husband ever abused the kids?
	Are you thinking of hurting yourself?

"Why" Questions	Open-Ended Questions That Replace "Why" Questions
Why did you ask him into your apartment?	How did things get out of control in your apartment?
Why did you smoke crack?	What was it like to decide to smoke crack?
Why did you try to kill yourself?	What was going through your mind when you took the pills?
How do these questions make you feel?	

Paraphrasing

Paraphrasing by the counselor can be done in two ways. Counselors can either restate in their own words what they thought they heard clients say, or they can clarify what was said in a questioning manner. The clarifying technique is used to clear up confusion or ambiguity and thus avoid misunderstanding and confirm the accuracy of what counselors heard. Clients are asked to rephrase or restate a previous message. This type of question is used for verification (i.e., making sure that what the crisis worker heard is what the client intended to say). The question is not meant to encourage clients to explore more of what was said, but simply to help counselors make sure that they understood what was said. Sometimes, clients talk in such a fragmented manner or so rapidly that important facts and ideas may not be heard accurately, and clarifying aids counselors in clearly understanding what was said.

Restating back to the client what the counselor heard is essential in building rapport and empathy. The crisis worker should not parrot or simply repeat exactly what the client said, but instead the goal is to share with the client what was heard by the counselor. The focus is on the cognitive and factual part of the client's message. The intent is to encourage elaboration of the statements to let the client know that you, the counselor, have understood or heard the message; to help the client focus on a specific situation, idea, or action; and to highlight content when attention to affect would be premature or inappropriate (Slaikeu, 1990, p. 38).

Exercise

Choose a partner, and ask a third person to be an observer. One person plays the crisis interviewer, and one plays a client in crisis. After the client tells the counselor about the crisis, the counselor is to restate in her own words what was heard. Do not parrot or repeat exactly what was said. Sometimes it is helpful for the counselor to break out of character and tell the observer, in the third person, what she heard the client say. The counselor can then go back into character and talk directly to the client, paraphrasing what she heard the client say. The dialogue shows how this might work:

> CLIENT: "I've been depressed since I had to have my dog put to sleep last week. I can't sleep or concentrate at work and everyone thinks I'm a big baby."

> CRISIS WORKER: "Are you saying that you have felt very bad since your dog died and aren't receiving any support from your coworkers?" (Clarifying)

> CRISIS WORKER: "I hear you saying that since putting your dog to sleep last week, you've been unable to sleep and feel depressed, and no one at work seems to understand your feelings." (Restatement)

Reflection of Feelings

Empathy is integral to achieving and maintaining contact with clients. This means being able to let clients know you understand their feelings. The technique of reflection, which is a statement that reflects the affective part or emotional tone of the client's message, whether verbal or nonverbal, is a powerful tool in creating an empathic environment. Not only does it help clarify the client's feelings in a particular situation, but it also helps the client feel understood. Clients can then express their own feelings about a situation; learn to manage their feelings, especially negative ones; and express their feelings toward the mental health care provider and agency. As we saw in Chapter 1, Caplan proposed that one characteristic of people who are coping effectively is their ability to express feelings freely and master them. Reflection of feelings allows such a process to occur.

Therapists from Freud to Rogers have believed that catharsis and experiential awareness of feelings are the curative factors in therapy. The crisis interview might be the only time the client has ever felt validated in her or his feelings, and that is a good experience!

Exercise

In pairs or in a group, have someone role-play a client in crisis, who will tell the others of his or her problem and feelings. Each student counselor then restates just the feelings to the client. Listen to the emotional tone and look for nonverbal cues, such as eyes watering or a fist pounding. Try using these openings: "You seem to feel . . . ," "Sounds as though you feel . . . ," "I sense you are . . . ." Look for ambivalent and contradictory feelings as well as positive feelings.

Here are some examples:

Painful feelings: "Sounds like you are furious with your wife."

Positive feelings: "You seem to be happiest when you don't drink."

Ambivalent feelings: "Although you say you hate your husband, you also seem to pity him."

Nonverbal feelings: "I can see by the tears in your eyes how painful this loss is."

Summarization

The key purpose of summarization is to help another individual pull his or her thoughts together. A secondary purpose is to check on whether you as a helper have distorted the client's frame of reference. Summarization may be helpful in beginning an interview if you've seen the client previously; it may help to bring together threads of data over several interviews or simply clarify what has gone on in the present interview (Ivey et al., 1997, p. 92). This is an example of a summarization: "So, your husband beat you last night and this time hit your daughter. You are scared and lonely and don't know where to turn."

The next section of the ABC model shows that summarization can help make a smooth transition from identifying the problem to finding coping strategies. Usually the cognitive and affective content are restated as well as the precipitating events and coping efforts. These aspects are easy to remember if you keep in mind the three aspects of any crisis: (1) the precipitating event; (2) the perception of the event by the client, which leads to subjective distress; and (3) failure of the client to cope successfully with the distress.

Now that you've learned the basic attending skills, practice them in 7- to 10-minute role-plays using the evaluation sheet in Table 5.1. Once you have mastered these skills, you are ready to move on to more advanced communication skills. The basic attending skills will be used throughout every session. They help counselors maintain rapport and allow them access to delicate information about the client. Counselors must use these basic attending skills during both the "B" and "C" stages of the ABC Model.

B: IDENTIFYING THE PROBLEM

After demographic information has been gathered and as rapport is developing, the crisis worker starts to focus on the client's presenting crisis. Identifying the problem is the second step in the ABC method and the most crucial one. Refer to the ABC Model of Crisis Intervention outline in Table 5.2 for a look at the interview process. Each aspect is examined individually as well as in the context of the others in the process. Beginning counselors should become so well-versed

TABLE 5.2 | **ABC MODEL OF CRISIS INTERVENTION**

	Skill Proficiency		
A: Developing and Maintaining Contact	Good	Fair	Poor
1. Attending behavior	_____	_____	_____
2. Questions	_____	_____	_____
3. Paraphrasing	_____	_____	_____
4. Reflection	_____	_____	_____
5. Summarization	_____	_____	_____
B. Identifying the Problem and Therapeutic Interaction	Assessed	Not Assessed	N/A
Identify the precipitating event	_____	_____	_____
Explore cognitions	_____	_____	_____
Identify emotional distress	_____	_____	_____
Identify impairments in functioning			
1. Behavioral	_____	_____	_____
2. Social	_____	_____	_____
3. Academic	_____	_____	_____
4. Occupational	_____	_____	_____
	Done	Not Done	N/A
Identify precrisis level of functioning	_____	_____	_____
Identify ethical issues			
1. Suicide assessment	_____	_____	_____
2. Child abuse, elder abuse, danger to others	_____	_____	_____
3. Organic or other medical concerns	_____	_____	_____
Identify substance abuse issues	_____	_____	_____
Use therapeutic interactions			
1. Educational comments	_____	_____	_____
2. Empowerment comments	_____	_____	_____
3. Validation and supportive comments	_____	_____	_____
4. Reframes	_____	_____	_____
C. Coping			
Identify client's current coping attempts	_____	_____	_____
Encourage client to think of other coping strategies	_____	_____	_____

TABLE 5.2 | CONTINUED

Present alternative coping ideas

1. Refer to support groups,   ———   ———   ———
   12-step groups
2. Refer to long-term therapy, family   ———   ———   ———
   therapy
3. Refer to medical doctor   ———   ———   ———
4. Refer to lawyer   ———   ———   ———
5. Refer to agency   ———   ———   ———
6. Suggest bibliotherapy, journaling,   ———   ———   ———
   "reel" therapy
7. Suggest other behavioral activities

Follow-up

in the various aspects of this model that they do not appear mechanical to the client. Keeping in mind the definition of crisis helps counselors remember what to identify: precipitating events, perceptions, subjective distress, and functioning.

Although the model is presented in a linear outline form, interviews do not have to be conducted in a linear fashion. Unfortunately for beginning counselors, having a script for each crisis situation is just not practical. However, the examples presented can be used in conjunction with the counselors' creative processes and intuition. This outline will be useful for you as you practice each type of crisis in subsequent chapters. In each of those chapters, examples are given for practice in role-playing. Do not be restricted to using only the ideas given. Create your own ideas whenever possible. The outline can be used for a 10-minute phone call, a 50-minute session, or a 6-week (or longer) series of crisis intervention sessions. Each week, new issues can be addressed and new coping strategies sought; also, changes in functioning can be assessed from week to week. Notice that the model has several areas to assess. This does not mean that on every visit the counselor must make an assessment for each area. Rather, each area should be addressed at least on the first or second visit and then reassessed thereafter as necessary to evaluate the client's progress.

Of particular importance in crisis intervention and in brief therapy is the ability to explore the client's perceptions. Most sessions will be spent in this process; and through these explorations clients gain knowledge of the source of their pain. Once clients' perceptions and frame of reference regarding various situations are understood, the crisis worker is in a position to guide clients into new ways of thinking and experiencing themselves and the world. Also, once clients' cognitions are changed, subjective distress will be reduced, coping skills can be implemented, and functioning will be increased. This, as you will recall, is the goal of crisis intervention.

The interview process can be thought of as climbing a tree with the client (see figure 5.1). The client will usually present with the precipitating event or subjective distress such as emotional pain or impairment in functioning. The

FIGURE 5.1 | THE COGNITION TREE

Cognition 1 Is a Branch
  [Twigs and leaves explore
  this cognition—leaves are
  brown (cognitive key)]

Cognition 2 Is a Branch
  [Twigs and leaves explore
  this cognition—leaves are
  brown (cognitive key)]

Cognition 3 Is a Branch
  [Twigs and leaves explore
  this cognition—leaves are
  brown (cognitive key)]

**Clients present a trunk:
a precipitating event,
emotions, or impairments
in functioning**

goal of the B section is to "climb the tree" to explore how all the components are related to the cognitions.

The counselor climbs up the trunk with the client by asking what the client's thoughts are about the trunk. These thoughts are explored by asking the client to further explain what the client means. Open-ended questions are used to help the client explore all related thoughts and perceptions until the leaves are understood—they are the cognitive key. The counselor can help change the leaves from brown to green with therapeutic interaction comments. Examples of therapeutic interaction comments can be found in many sections of subsequent chapters and will be defined clearly later in this chapter. Many times, several important cognitions are presented. Each one will have to be explored and new therapeutic comments then provided. Identifying cognitions and offering new ways of thinking about the situation is the main focus of any crisis intervention session.

By exploring the many limbs and twigs of the initial perception presented, the counselor and client gain a deeper understanding of what is really bothering the client most about the precipitating event. It often takes as many as six questions before the cognitive key can be established and therapeutic statements offered. If the counselor attempts to provide an educational statement, a reframe, a support statement, or an empowerment statement too soon, the client often resists. The client probably just needed more time to fully explain his or her cognitive tree. Below is a sample dialogue in which therapist and client climb the tree:

CLIENT: "My husband left me." (Presents a precipitating event)

COUNSELOR: "What does that mean to you?" (Asks open-ended question to explore perception)

CLIENT: "I will be alone forever." (First cognition presented; client thinks she'll be alone forever)

COUNSELOR: "In what way alone?" (Counselor tries to understand exactly what client means by "alone")

CLIENT: "No one will ever love me again." (New cognitive statement)

COUNSELOR: "What makes you think that?"

CLIENT: "He told me that he's the only one who could ever love me because I'm so ugly and stupid." (More new information about the original cognition)

COUNSELOR: "What are your thoughts about the idea of your being ugly and stupid?"

CLIENT: "Well, I don't think I'm really that stupid."

COUNSELOR: "What do you think?'

CLIENT: "I'm afraid to be alone and start all over."

COUNSELOR: "What is most scary for you about this?"

CLIENT: "I'm afraid to get close to someone else and feel hurt."

COUNSELOR: "It is often scary to start over." (Support statement that validates client's feelings and thoughts) "This scary feeling may at some point turn into excitement at the opportunity to have a more rewarding relationship." (A brief reframe of the scariness possibly being excitement)

At this point, the client may feel some hope and her cognitions will probably have changed to some extent. Notice how many questions were necessary to reach the deeper meanings behind her initial cognition.

Probably the most important reason for exploring the client's internal frame of reference is that changing internal perceptions is easier than changing external situations. If the crisis worker spends too much time focusing on the significant others and the details of the situation—elements that generally cannot be changed—the client may experience increased frustration.

At the end of this chapter, a "script" using the ABC model of crisis intervention is presented. It offers specific questions and statements a crisis worker might use. It is presented after readers have had a chance to learn about each section of the model individually. Then they should be able to understand how to integrate all the sections in a typical interview.

Identifying the Precipitating Event

Shortly after the interview begins, the counselor should begin to ask about the precipitating event. To ask, "What happened that made you call for an appointment?" is appropriate. It is an opening for clients to tell what is going on with them. If clients cannot think of any particular event that brought them to counseling, the crisis worker must probe further, explaining that understanding the trigger of a client's crisis aids in relieving the crisis state.

The precipitating event may have happened yesterday or 6 weeks ago. A helpful strategy is learning when the client started to feel bad, which helps pinpoint the triggering event. "The straw that broke the camel's back" is a common expression that can help clients focus on the beginning of the crisis.

Another reason for specifying the precipitating event is to be able, later on, to explore how the client has been trying to cope since it happened. When the client's denial is strong, the crisis worker must confront the client about why exactly the client decided to come for counseling. The reason is usually because of difficulty in coping with a precipitating event. If the event is not clearly defined, the counselor will have problems presenting alternative coping strategies to deal with the event. Last, identification of the precipitating event is vital because the crisis worker must identify the client's perceptions about the episode. If these cognitions are not identified properly, there can be no therapeutic interactive comments related to them. Remember, change in the way the event is perceived is essential to increasing the functioning level of clients. In Chapter 1, two formulas were presented and are repeated here. Refer to them as you practice using the ABC model.

Formula for Understanding the Process of Crisis Formation

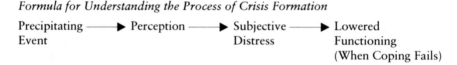

If the goal of crisis work is to increase clients' functioning, the following formula aids crisis workers in understanding how to move clients out of a crisis.

Formula to Increase Functioning

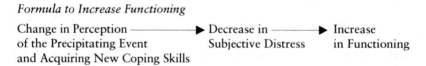

No matter how much clients profess that "nothing has happened, really," something drove them to seek help. Squeeze it out of them! They need to see that their current state of subjective distress is tied to an actual event or fact.

Recognizing the Meaning or Perception of the Precipitating Event

In addition to identifying precipitating events, crisis workers need to actively explore the meaning clients ascribe to these events. It is clients' perceptions of stressful situations that cause them to be in a crisis state as well as the inability to cope with the stress. Usually, stress originates from one of four areas: loss of control, loss of self-esteem, loss of nurturance, or forced adjustment to a change in life or role. The meaning behind these losses is helpful to explore.

All aspects of the situation should be examined. For example, suppose a woman is raped. Not only does the actual rape cause stress, but her perception of how her husband will react also contributes to her stress as she struggles with her perceived new role with him.

Some questions the crisis worker may ask to elicit the client's frame of reference regarding the crisis situation include these: "How do you put it together in your head?" "What do you think about this?" "What does it mean to you that . . . ?" "What are you telling yourself about . . . ?" "What assumptions are you making about . . . ?"

Cognitive restructuring or reframing is a valuable tool for the counselor but can be done only if the client's current cognitions are known. It is impossible to develop a coping plan for clients without examining the cognitive and perceptual experience. Think of yourself as a mechanic who needs to analyze and experience the trouble firsthand before tinkering with the engine.

Assessing the client's perception of the precipitating event is the most important part of the interview and must be done thoroughly on every visit to check for changing views as well as long-standing views on a variety of issues.

Identifying Subjective Distress and Functioning Level

In addition to exploring stressors and clients' perceptions of them, counselors must inquire about clients' functioning and how the precipitating events are affecting it. Clients seem to benefit from expressing painful feelings and sharing other symptoms—symptoms that may impair clients' occupational, academic, behavioral, social, interpersonal, or family functioning. Counselors should ask how clients' perceptions about the precipitating event are affecting their functioning in each area.

Often each area in which the person is suffering distress is dealt with separately because a specific perception may be associated with that area and not another. The crisis worker is advised to explore each area affected during the crisis state in as much detail as possible. This probing gives the counselor a feel for the degree of impairment the client is experiencing and can be used later to help select coping strategies. When clients discuss their symptoms and impairments in functioning, they can receive feedback, education, and support from the counselor. Often, understanding one's feelings and behaviors is the first step in coping with them.

> **Example:** A battered woman might be experiencing much anxiety at work because she believes that her husband will come there and cause a scene, which would probably result in her being fired. This perception might be dealt with by letting her know that bosses can often be sympathetic and helpful, and that her boss might even provide her with support and initiate legal action for her.

In addition to identifying the client's current level of functioning, the crisis worker needs to assess the client's precrisis level of functioning in order to compare the two. This will help the counselor determine the level of coping the client can realistically achieve; it also gives the counselor an idea of the severity of the crisis for the person. The comparison serves as a basis for evaluating the outcome of crisis intervention. Remember that the goal of crisis intervention is to bring the client back to the precrisis level of functioning.

> **Example:** If a woman was getting straight As in college before being raped, and afterward her grades went down to Cs and Ds, her crisis was worse for her than for a woman who was raped but showed only minimal disturbance at work or school. In these cases, it is probable that the first woman's perception of the rape was more drastic than the second woman's. Maybe she told herself that she was at fault, that she is dirty, and that no one will ever love her again. The second woman might have a more realistic view of the rape and be able to tell herself that it was the rapist's fault and that no one is going to hold her responsible or think differently about her.

Most intake forms ask for a comparison between current and previous functioning on a regular basis. It is important to include this information as part of any crisis assessment procedure.

Making Ethical Checks

Several other areas need identification at this stage of the interview. These have ethical implications and must be assessed either directly or indirectly with every client. However, in order not to behave like a prosecuting attorney, the crisis worker is encouraged to extract this information in a fluid, relevant manner. Rather than going down a list and asking one question after another, the counselor should weave the questions in as the issues arise in the normal flow of the conversation.

Suicide Check Because people in crisis are vulnerable and often confused and overwhelmed, suicide sometimes becomes an alternative for them. Every crisis worker must assess for suicidality, particularly when the client is depressed or impulsive. Suicide assessment and prevention are discussed in detail in Chapter 6.

Homicidal/Abuse Issues As discussed in the ethics chapter, mental health workers in many states are required to report child and elder abuse and any suspicion that a client may harm someone. Assessment of these issues must be done during the course of an interview. Often, the counselor's intuition will provide the basis for detailed inquiry. Child abuse and elder abuse are dealt with in subsequent chapters; working with clients who are a danger to others is examined in Chapter 6.

> **Example:** A 43-year-old male may say that he hates his father for having beaten his mother and can see himself smashing the father's face. This statement alone does not warrant an attempt to take the client into custody. However, I would inquire how he deals with this anger, especially toward his wife and children. It is important for counselors to know that suspected abuse of children must be assessed in all cases. Sometimes, turning away and collaborating in denial with an abusive family is easier than facing the issue, but doing so is never in the best interest of the child. Such action is unethical and might be illegal, depending on the laws of the state where the action occurs.

> **Example:** The mother of a 15-year-old boy and a 16-year-old girl is in a crisis state and seeks help from a counselor. Two weeks earlier, the husband whipped the boy

with a belt and left welts on his back. The father also slapped the girl across the face. When the mother was informed by the crisis worker that a child abuse report would have to be made, she was very upset and pleaded with the therapist not to make the report. She thought that it would affect her getting a high-security job for which she was applying; would make the husband angry; and would cause anxiety for her son, who was worried that his dad would take his car away. The counselor explained that a report was mandatory in this situation. To alleviate the mother's concern, the counselor made the report in the presence of the clients, so they would know what would most likely happen according to the social worker taking the call.

Making clients part of the reporting process helped them deal with it in a less fearful manner. The counselor had no choice but to make the report, even though the clients did not want her to.

Organic or Other Concerns   If clients state that they suffer from serious depression, bipolar disorder, obsessive-compulsive disorder, or schizophrenia, they should already be receiving medication. Crisis workers should assess for medication compliance for these cases and encourage noncompliant clients to continue with prescribed medication until they can schedule an appointment with their physician. In these situations, crisis workers may want to consult with the physician by phone to ensure that clients receive the most effective treatment. When clients describe or exhibit behaviors, symptoms, or complaints that may be due to biological factors such as Alzheimer's disease or attention deficit disorder with hyperactivity (ADHD) but have not yet been formally diagnosed with a serious disorder, crisis workers should refer them to a physician or psychiatrist for further assessment.

Substance Abuse Issues

Checking for substance abuse on a regular basis is a good idea and is often part of the intake form in most agencies. Because clients involved with substance use and abuse often deny and minimize their use, the crisis worker needs to be somewhat assertive in gathering information about drug use. Following are some examples showing how to extract this information without offending clients:

"Tell me about your past and present drug and alcohol use."

This statement assumes that use exists or existed and is stated matter-of-factly, as if you won't be shocked to hear of it. The person who has not used drugs can simply say "None."

"How much alcohol do you use a week?"

"What other drugs besides cocaine do you use or have you used?"

These questions do not seem to be as judgmental or grilling as the following do:

"Do you use alcohol? Do you use cocaine? Do you smoke pot? Do you drink daily?"

Using general, open-ended questions will save time and reduce defensiveness in clients.

Therapeutic Interaction

The main part of the session, and probably the most therapeutic part, will be spent in identifying the client's beliefs and feelings, and then providing supportive statements, educational information, empowering statements, and reframing statements that will aid the client in thinking differently about the situation and assist them in coping with it. Of course, active listening skills remain important, but once these are mastered, the counselor is ready to use the more advanced skills discussed next to help clients improve their coping ability.

Validation and Support Statements   The counselor may, from time to time, tell clients that their feelings are normal or suggest there is hope that things will get better. In response to a woman who has just found out that her husband has been molesting their daughter and feels as though the world has come to an end, a crisis worker might respond supportively by saying, "I know that right now you feel that everything is falling apart, but many people have gone through the same situation and have survived. You have every reason to believe you can survive, too."

Support statements are not false hopes or words like "It'll be OK," "Don't worry," or "Forget about it." These comments are typical of family and friends who mean well; however, they are not very useful. As crisis workers, we need to say things to people that others do not say. Also, because clients see counselors as experts in crisis situations, they will tend to take comfort in supportive comments from these helpers, often adopting a more optimistic attitude. Receiving validation from a counselor about one's feelings can help clients not see themselves as sick, weak, or bad.

Educational Statements   Providing factual information, whether developmental or situational, is vital in every crisis. Clients often suffer merely because they lack, or have incorrect, knowledge about the precipitating event and aspects associated with it. Thus, it is imperative for crisis workers to gather as much information as possible about each crisis situation. Whether this is done through formal academic courses, books, experience, or supervision, it gives counselors an edge in helping clients work through their issues.

Educational statements may include psychological, social, and interpersonal dynamics, or they may provide statistics or frequency of the problem. In any case, when a counselor helps people in a crisis state increase their knowledge of facts, the clients will have stronger coping skills for the current crisis and future crises. You will remember from Chapter 1 that seeking reality and information was one of Caplan's characteristics of effective coping behavior.

Picture a woman who has been completely isolated from others because she is in an ongoing battering relationship. She will most likely perceive herself as abnormal and bizarre. When she learns that about 30 percent of women live in such relationships, she may feel differently about herself and the abnormality of the situation. Without this issue to deal with, the counselor is now free to process other issues.

Empowering Statements   Clients who are in certain crisis situations in which they feel violated, victimized, or helpless respond well to empowering statements. Clients are presented with choices and are encouraged to take back personal power by making good choices. Battered women, rape survivors, and survivors of child abuse often suffer from learned helplessness stemming from the abuse. They feel that they cannot prevent bad things from happening because, in the past, they could not prevent abuse by a physically stronger (or in some other way stronger) perpetrator. This perception often motivates them to survive abuse rather than try and escape from it. A useful strategy is to let clients know that they may not have had the choice to stop the abuse from happening at an earlier time but that now they certainly can make choices to do something about the abuse (e.g., press charges, confront the perpetrator, talk about it). Also, the crisis worker can point out that they do not have to choose certain behaviors. It is important that they move from a position of feeling powerless to feeling that they have some control and choice in their life now.

> **Example:** A rape victim might be told, "You didn't have a choice in being raped, but now you do have a choice of what to do. You can call the police, go to counseling, tell a friend, or not do any of these things. Let's talk about your feelings and thoughts on each of these choices."

Reframing Statements   In its simplest form, reframing is defining a situation differently from the way the client is defining it. It is a cognitive restructuring tactic that aims at changing the crisis from danger to opportunity. American clichés such as "Every cloud has a silver lining" and "When life gives you lemons, make lemonade" convey this idea quite clearly.

Reframing may seem like rationalizing away a problem to some. However, it is probably one of the strongest healing skills available to the crisis worker and for people in general. It allows us to acknowledge that life is a struggle, that we aren't perfect, and that dwelling on our failings is not necessary or helpful. Instead, if we can believe that something positive or beneficial will be an outcome or result of the problem, we can usually integrate the difficult episode more easily. The crisis worker's responsibility is to be creative in finding the right reframe, which means actively searching for the positive. Reframing is an advanced technique that puts problems in a solvable form by changing the meanings of behaviors and situations and providing a new perspective that opens up new possibilities for change.

> **Example:** The author worked with a woman whose rape case was rejected by the district attorney after she had hoped for a year that it would go to court. The rapist was free, and her victimization had not been acknowledged because of a legal technicality. The counselor and client could have both thrown up their hands, called the judicial system names, and seethed internally. Alternatively, the counselor pointed out to the client that the rape prodded her to seek counseling that allowed her not only to work through the rape issues but also to identify her codependency and its effects on her relationships. This knowledge led the way to better family relations and intimacy with her boyfriend. The reframe was that the rape, although terrifying, had been survived and indirectly allowed for an opportunity

to gain self-understanding and growth. This client could tolerate this reframe because she had undergone one year of intensive therapy and had strong rapport with the counselor, who truly understood the client's frame of reference.

Reframing is possible only if the counselor first understands fully the client's current frame of reference. Otherwise, the counselor would not know what should be reframed. Counselors can learn the client's frame of reference by asking direct questions: "How do you perceive the situation?" "What does it mean to you?" "What runs through your head about it?" Reframing is not a technique to be taken lightly, and careful supervision is necessary in learning its effective use. Sometimes reframing is associated with a cold, strategic approach, but it can be done in an authentic, caring manner. The counselor does not deny the seriousness of the problem but instead offers a way out of a problem that allows the person to preserve the integrity of the self and often the family unit as well. Because reframes are usually offered with the person's self-identity in mind, shame is reduced and self-integrity is preserved. The examples of reframes provided in each of the following sections show this principle of self-preservation clearly.

In summary, the B section of the ABC model can be thought of as identifying issues one at a time and providing various forms of feedback as the process moves forward to a place where the client can accept coping as viable behavior. Periodically, the crisis worker should summarize the precipitating events, the client's perceptions of them, the client's functioning in several areas of life, and any major symptoms of concern.

C: COPING

The last step of the ABC model is concerned with the client's coping behavior—past, present, and future. Past coping success can be built on to help the person weather the present and future difficulties.

Exploring the Client's Own Attempts at Coping

Toward the conclusion of an interview, counselors should begin summing up the problem and moving clients into a coping mode. To do this, crisis workers ask clients how they have managed crises in the past. All coping, whether it is helpful or not, should be examined. In this way, clients can make a mental list of what works and what does not.

If the client cannot think of any past coping behavior, the crisis worker should be very encouraging. The counselor might say, "Well, you must have done something or you would not have made it this far." Remember that even sleeping and social withdrawal are coping strategies, and the counselor and client should talk about their helpfulness or unhelpfulness. Eliciting unhealthy attempts at coping is especially valuable as it helps the client see what has not worked in the past. The client will generally be more open to alternatives once the ineffectiveness of his or her current behavior is made evident.

Encouraging the Development of New Coping Behaviors

After current coping attempts have been discussed, the counselor can prod clients to ponder other possible ways of coping. The crisis worker can ask clients how they think they can proceed at this point to begin to get out of the crisis state. Remember that clients have already been presented with educational information, reframes, supportive comments, and empowerment statements. It is time for clients to do some of their own thinking. Clients are more likely to follow through with a plan they have developed themselves than with one suggested by the counselor. It is appropriate for a counselor to be challenging and persistent in getting clients to think of ways they could begin to cope better. This approach helps clients get in touch with their problem-solving abilities.

Presenting Alternative Coping Behaviors

Clients should be allowed first to propose their own methods for coping with their problems. When they have reached the end of the resources they know, however, the counselor should suggest other options. Many of these may be completely new to clients, offering them fresh insights. The suggestions offered by the counselor should be based on previous discussions with the client. The client will often provide the counselor with the best alternative for that particular client. For example, a client might have said that one of the things that made her feel better was talking to her girlfriends about her divorce. But now, she says, they are tired of listening. This should trigger in the counselor the idea that this client feels better talking to a group of women about her problem. Getting the client to accept a referral to a support group should not be difficult, because the client herself has said that doing this type of thing has already made her feel better!

Support Groups and 12-Step Groups   If support systems haven't already been discussed, now is a good time to identify some existing natural support, such as coworkers, supervisors, relatives, friends, schoolmates, or church members. Clients may not have considered any of these people as helpers in getting through the crisis. With a little encouragement, they may be persuaded to reach out to others. This is not to suggest that crisis workers should avoid giving support to clients. However, it is often more comfortable for clients to receive help from natural support systems than to rely on mental health professionals during crises. As Caplan (1964) suggested earlier, people who are coping effectively with a situation will actively ask others for help, not necessarily mental health workers. The idea of encouraging clients to help themselves parallels the adage of teaching a man to fish versus just giving him fish. Self-sufficiency is more economical in the long run. I have often felt that as a crisis interventionist, my job is to put myself out of a job by encouraging clients to function on their own and with the support of others in their life. A crisis worker is merely a beacon shedding light on these resources.

Some clients may need referrals to 12-step groups such as Alcoholics Anonymous (AA), Al-Anon, Co-Dependents Anonymous, Cocaine Anonymous, or others. These mutual self-help groups are free and have no time limits for attendance; sessions can be found in every city at various hours of the day. The trend now is for insurance companies to pay for only 6–12 sessions of therapy, so 12-step groups are a lifesaver for many people who cannot afford to pay for therapy out of their own pockets.

Long-Term Therapy, Marital Therapy, and Family Therapy   Some clients' problems have been going on for so long that crisis intervention cannot resolve them. Perhaps because of a personality disorder or other chronic emotional disorder, clients need ongoing therapy with a trained professional. This might be individual therapy or marital or family therapy. Often, a crisis is an opportunity for clients to resolve long-term problems that have been hidden for many years.

Shelters and Other Agencies   To address other problems, crisis workers need to be knowledgeable about community agencies and resources. Clients who are anxious and feeling overwhelmed are more likely to follow through with a referral when it is presented in written form with choices, addresses, phone numbers, and fees. Providing written information is much more effective than telling clients to look for certain services in the Yellow Pages. Even if you are conducting a phone interview, having these resources in hand, separated by the type of crisis, certainly aids the expediency of referral. Also, crisis workers will know whether an agency can actually help a client at an affordable rate if workers have recently updated their information about the agency.

Most communities have community resource directories that list various agencies, and local libraries also have listings available. One of the best ways to get names of agencies is by contacting an agency that has similar services. Most mental health and social service agencies are familiar with agencies in the community.

A useful assignment for beginning crisis intervention students is to do research on various community agencies and resources that regularly intervene in crisis situations. It is amazing to learn how many resources are available in most communities for almost any crisis situation. Community resources were developed during the grassroots era of the 1960s, and they have evolved over the years into an elaborate networking system of many different agencies. Large organizations often have nationwide toll-free phone numbers that workers can call to get information about many agencies. The organizations serve as clearinghouses for a variety of resources. Some examples of community resources include local churches, local community colleges, county mental health agencies, local AA groups, and private clubs such as the Sierra Club.

Some resources are more appropriate for certain crises than others. Suicidal clients should be given a list of hotlines to call, if necessary, between sessions. Persons suffering a loss from divorce might be referred to a divorce recovery workshop through a church or support group. Clients dealing with issues related to HIV or AIDS should be referred to a local AIDS services foundation for support groups. It is widely known that substance abusers and their significant others benefit from 12-step groups such as AA or Al-Anon. Sexual assault victims and battered women benefit from a referral to shelters or specialized support groups.

At times, crisis workers may want to contact an agency and let someone there know about a referral. It is quite reasonable to ask for a follow-up call or note about whether the client used the resource. In other instances, a client may return to a crisis worker for another individual session and the crisis worker at that time can ask whether the client attended the support group or used the service recommended.

Medical and Legal Referrals   In some cases, medical or legal referrals are necessary. Even crisis workers who are considered paraprofessionals should have an understanding of the legal, political, and medical systems and how they will make an impact on various types of crises. For instance, workers should know the conditions under which a police officer may arrest a battering spouse. Also, they should have knowledge of restraining orders, which may be useful for a victim of abuse. How the court system generally deals with rape or child abuse is useful information as well. Though they are not expected to be lawyers, crisis workers need to keep abreast of recent laws that affect clients in crisis.

Similarly, though they are not expected or allowed to be physicians, crisis workers need to be able to refer someone to a doctor for an evaluation when medication or other treatment might be useful. Learning to consult and work with medical doctors is a skill worth developing, and knowing when to make a referral to a physician is vital.

Bibliotherapy, Journaling, and Reel Therapy   Every crisis worker needs to have some knowledge of reading material for clients in a variety of crisis situations. Using these materials with clients is called bibliotherapy. Reading often provides a new way of looking at the crisis (reframing) and gives the client information and support—especially books written by a person who has gone through a similar crisis. For example, reading a book by a woman who was raped will help the recently raped woman see that her feelings are normal; this knowledge should have a calming effect. Also, reading helps people think rather than feel, encouraging more productive problem-solving activity. Having clients keep a journal of their thoughts is also quite helpful; the clients may discover new feelings and thoughts as they jot them down on paper. The journal may be shared with the counselor or remain private.

Many therapists are also using movies to help move their clients toward breakthroughs more quickly. Viewing movies allows clients to "grow" in their own "free" time. For example, Nielsen (quoted in Hesley, 2000, pp. 55–57) has used the movie *Distant Thunder* for clients experiencing posttraumatic stress disorder. He states that many of his clients find it easier to explain their own "flashbacks" and "social phobia" after viewing this film. The use of films—so-called reel therapy—is likely to become more common because many future therapists watch films as part of their graduate school studies. Films do have limitations and should not take the place of personal discussion with the counselor. Movies should be selected carefully and thoughtfully (Hesley, 2000, pp. 55–57).

Other Behavioral Activities   Some clients may benefit from assertiveness training, in which the counselor teaches them how to ask for what they want, express feelings and needs to others, or set boundaries with others. Other tasks may include having clients exercise, visit friends and family, or engage in a recreational activity such as going to the beach.

All of these types of coping referrals provide ways for the client to cope and think differently about the precipitating event.

Commitment and Follow-Up

Part of making any referral or suggestion is commitment and follow-up, that is, counselors get a commitment from clients that they will indeed follow through with recommendations. This explains why it is best for clients to develop their own coping plans; they are more likely to follow through with a plan they have formulated themselves. In some cases, as with highly suicidal clients, a written contract may be prudent. The no-suicide contract is a useful intervention that will be discussed in a later chapter. Written contracts are often used with clients who need to control their impulses or with acting-out teenagers. Both the therapist and the client keep a copy of the contract and discuss it at the next session.

In sum, the C part of the ABC model first asks clients to explore current, past, and possibly new coping strategies to deal with the crisis at hand. Then the crisis worker offers alternative ideas, makes referrals, and asks clients for a commitment to follow through on the plan. The worker's hope is that clients will move from a dysfunctional state to a higher level of functioning and perceived control over the precipitating event. At each visit, the crisis worker can verify and suggest connecting with these various coping aids, which gives clients something concrete to take home.

KEY TERMS FOR STUDY

attending behavior: Behavior that has to do with following the client's lead, actively listening, and demonstrating presence.

bibliotherapy: The use of books as an alternative coping strategy.

bipolar disorder: A condition in which states of manic behavior (i.e., out-of-control, hyper, grandiose behavior) fluctuate with states of extreme depression. It is sometimes known as manic-depression.

close-ended question: A type of question that can be answered with a "yes" or a "no" or some other one-word answer. Its best use is for obtaining facts such as age, number of children, or number of years married. Forced-choice questions, or "do you, have you" questions, are generally not effective. These types of questions can bring the interview to a dead end or sound like an interrogation.

commitment and follow-up: Verbal agreement given by client to a crisis worker at the end of a crisis intervention session. Specifically, it is what the client is going to do after leaving the session to deal with the crisis. It may include returning to see the same counselor or going elsewhere. Remember that the person in crisis is vulnerable and needs direction.

depression: A state of being in which the client is sad, low in energy, and suicidal; he or she feels worthless, helpless, and hopeless; the person lacks desire, is socially withdrawn, and is slowed in processes such as thinking and concentrating. This person should be referred to a physician for an evaluation.

educational statements: Types of therapeutic comments in which facts, statistics, and theories are presented to clients in an attempt to normalize their experience and change their misconceptions.

empowering statements: Therapeutic comments that help clients feel more in control and see choices they have. They are especially useful for clients who have been victimized.

hallucinations: False sensory perceptions. Auditory hallucinations are associated with schizophrenia; visual and tactile ones with substance abuse withdrawal; and gustatory and olfactory ones with organic brain disorders. Any hallucination is indicative of severe illness; when hallucinations are present, a doctor should be consulted.

legal or medical referrals: Referrals made by the crisis worker if the client needs the services of other professionals, as when a person has been arrested, wants a restraining order, or has a severe mental or other illness.

organic brain disorder: A condition resulting from a neurological disturbance, genetic abnormality, or tumor.

paraphrasing: A basic attending skill, or clarifying technique, in which counselors restate in their own words what was just said by the client.

rapport: A special type of bonding that a counselor seeks with a client. The more rapport there is between client and counselor, the greater the client's sense of trust and security.

reel therapy: The use of movies to aid clients in understanding and resolving their own issues.

reflection: The best way to show emotional empathy for a client; the counselor points out the client's emotions by stating them as either seen or heard.

reframing: A therapeutic restatement of a problem that helps the client see the situation differently, usually in a way that makes it easier to solve.

resources: Sources of help in the community. A crisis worker must be knowledgeable about community resources to be able to connect a client in crisis with the appropriate support group or other service.

schizophrenia: A disorder usually requiring the attention of a psychiatrist and characterized by the following symptoms: hallucinations, delusions, loose associations, blunt affect, and poor appearance.

support statements: Therapeutic statements that make clients feel validated and that the counselor truly understands and empathizes with their situation.

support systems: Networks of helping individuals and agencies. A crisis worker uses the client's natural support systems, such as family and friends, and also helps the client build new support systems.

summarization: A skill useful in tying ideas together, wrapping up a session, or moving from the B phase of the ABC model to the C phase; the skill is also useful when the counselor does not know where to go next. It is a statement that pulls together the various facts and feelings discussed in the session.

To sum up the ABC model, a sample script is presented in Table 5.3. This gives readers an idea of the types of questions to ask and statements to make when using the ABC model. The steps of the model are repeated in the table. In each section, please note the specific words (italicized) that a counselor might say to a client.

TABLE 5.3 | ABC MODEL OF CRISIS INTERVENTION (SAMPLE SCRIPT)

A: BASIC ATTENDING SKILLS

What brings you in today? You seem to be having a little trouble getting started. So your girlfriend told you she wants to break up last week and things haven't been going too well lately. You look like you are very sad.

B: IDENTIFYING THE PROBLEM AND THERAPEUTIC INTERACTION

Identify the Precipitating Event:

What specifically brought you in today? Did something happen recently, something different?

Explore Meanings, Cognitions, and Perceptions:

How do you think about it? What does it mean to you? What thoughts go through your mind when you picture the event? How do you put it together in your head? What is it like for you? What specifically do you mean? What are your perceptions about it (the precipitating event)?

Identify Subjective Distress (Emotional Distress):

How do you feel? What emotions are going on inside you? You seem sad, angry, ambivalent, in pain. How have you been feeling since (the precipitating event)?

Identify Impairments in Functioning in the Following Areas:

1. Behavioral
How have you been doing in your life? How are you sleeping? How is your appetite? Have you been carrying on with your normal activities?

2. Social
How are your relationships with your friends and family? Have you been seeing anyone socially since (the precipitating event)? How do you feel or act around people?

3. Academic
Are you going to school? How are your grades lately? Have you been able to study and concentrate in classes? How are you getting along with classmates?

4. Occupational
How are you doing at work? Has your work performance changed since (the precipitating event)? Have you been able to function adequately at work?

Identify Precrisis Level of Functioning in 1–4 above.

How has your ability to function socially, at school, and at work changed since (the precipitating event)? What was it like for you before (the precipitating event)? What/how were your relationships before (the precipitating event)?

TABLE 5.3 | CONTINUED

Identify Any Ethical Concerns:

1. Suicide assessment

Have you been thinking about hurting yourself? Have you attempted to kill yourself? Do you want to commit suicide? Do you have a plan? Do you have the means? What is stopping you from killing yourself?

2. Child abuse, elder abuse, homicide

Are your children in danger? Have you or your husband ever caused physical harm to your children? How hard do you hit your kids? How often do you leave your child alone? Have your kids gone without food for an entire day? Has your elderly parent been hurt by the retirement home? When did you first learn that your sister was stealing from your father? How often do you have thoughts about killing your wife? Have you ever hurt someone in the past? How strong are your feelings of murder?

3. Organic or other medical concerns

Are you able to get up in the morning and feed yourself? How many hours do you sleep? Can you dress yourself every day? Do you ever hear voices? Does it ever feel like the phone wires are talking to you? Do you have special powers? Can people read your mind or put thoughts into your head? Do you think people are out to get you? Do you smell or taste things that are unusual?

Identify Substance Abuse Issues:

What kinds of drugs have you used in the past? How much alcohol do you drink per week/month/day? What drugs do you use recreationally?

Use Therapeutic Interactions:

1. Educational comments

- *Although you feel as though you are the only woman who stays in a battering relationship, it is estimated that about 30 percent of women in the United States live in ongoing battering relationships. Going through a period of intense anger is quite normal and to be expected after the death of a loved one.*
- *Actually, it is not uncommon to be raped by someone you know. Date rape is extremely common for women ages 15–24.*
- *Studies to date do not show that one can catch HIV by shaking hands.*
- *It is not uncommon for the spouse of an alcoholic to be highly anxious about the spouse's drinking.*

2. Empowerment statements

- *It is true that you did not have a choice about being raped, but you do have choices now, including whether to press charges, get a medical exam, or drop the whole matter.*
- *Unfortunately, you cannot control your wife's drug use, but you can control your own behavior with her.*
- *True, you are HIV infected and cannot change that. You can, however, choose how to live the rest of your life.*

3. Support statements

- *This is an extremely difficult situation, and I don't take it lightly. I can only imagine the pain you are going through. I am so sorry this happened to you.*
- *Please, let me be there for you; I care. It must feel pretty bad if you want to kill yourself. These kinds of traumas often make people feel like giving up.*

TABLE 5.3 | CONTINUED

4. Reframes
I think it takes a lot of strength to cry, and I don't see crying as a sign of weakness. Although you see suicide as a sign of strength, it is actually the easy way out of a life filled with difficulties for us all. Staying with a batterer for the sake of your children is evidence of your strength, not a sign of weakness. (Please see each chapter for more examples of reframing.)

C: COPING

Identify Client's Current Coping Attempts:

What have you done to try to feel better? What else have you done? Anything else?

Encourage Client to Think of Other Coping Strategies:

What else can you think of to try to get through this? What have you done in the past to get through difficult times? What would you tell a friend to do in this case?

Present Alternative Coping Ideas:

1. Refer to support groups, 12-step groups
You said you feel better when you talk to friends; how would you feel about attending a support group with other people in your situation? I know of a very special group where people going through what you are going through meet to learn ways to deal with it. Will you give it a try? You can go for as long as you need to, and it is free.

2. Refer to long-term therapy, family therapy
I believe you could benefit most by going to a family therapist/marital therapist. Would you consider this? It appears that your problems are longstanding. I think longer-term therapy would be really good for you. I know several great counselors. I'll give you a list.

3. Refer to medical doctor or psychiatrist
I would feel most comfortable if you would see a physician. Your symptoms seem serious, and you may need medication or a physical. Do you know of a doctor, or shall I refer you to one that I really respect and work with on other cases?

4. Legal referral
I think you should get legal advice from an attorney. These matters are beyond my scope of expertise. Please go to the public defender today or tomorrow. Are you aware of restraining orders? You can find out about them at the district attorney's office.

5. Refer to shelter, other agency
How would you feel about going to a battered woman's/homeless shelter? You will be safe there.

6. Recommend books and keeping a journal
Do you like to read? I know of some really good books that help explain more about what you are going through. Here is a list of books I recommend for you to read. You said you like to write and have kept a diary before. Many clients feel more under control if they keep a journal while going through difficult times.

Obtain Commitment; Do Follow-up:

When can you make another appointment with me? Call me when you set up your appointment with Dr. Jones. I am going to call you tomorrow. Will you promise not to hurt yourself until you at least speak to me first?

II

PTSD, COMMUNITY DISASTERS, AND TRAUMA RESPONSE

POSTTRAUMATIC STRESS DISORDER (PTSD)

Posttraumatic stress disorder (PTSD) is a broad category that applies to people who have been severely traumatized at one or more times in their lives; at present, they are not functioning effectively because they have not integrated the trauma and laid it to rest. The cause is exposure to a situation perceived to be threatening to oneself or one's loved ones.

The American Psychiatric Association's *Diagnostic and Statistical Manual of Mental Disorders, Fourth Edition, Text Revision* (DSM-IV-TR) (1994) defines PTSD this way:

A. The person has been exposed to a traumatic event in which both of the following were present:

  1. The person experienced, witnessed, or was confronted with an event or events that involved actual or threatened death or serious injury, or a threat to the physical integrity of self or others.

  2. The person's response involved intense fear, helplessness, or horror. **Note:** In children, this may be expressed instead by disorganized or agitated behavior.

B. The traumatic event is persistently reexperienced in one (or more) of the following ways:

  1. Recurrent and intrusive distressing recollections of the event, including images, thoughts, or perceptions. **Note:** In young

children, repetitive play may occur in which themes or aspects of the trauma are expressed.

2. Recurrent distressing dreams of the event. **Note:** In children, there may be frightening dreams without recognizable content.

3. Acting or feeling as if the traumatic event were recurring (includes a sense of reliving the experience, illusions, hallucinations, and **dissociative** flashback episodes, including those that occur on awakening or when intoxicated). Note: In young children, trauma-specific reenactment may occur.

4. Intense psychological distress at exposure to internal or external cues that symbolize or resemble an aspect of the traumatic event.

5. Physiological reactivity on exposure to internal or external cues that symbolize or resemble an aspect of the traumatic event.

C. Persistent avoidance of stimuli associated with the trauma and numbing of general responsiveness (not present before the trauma), as indicated by three (or more) of the following:

1. efforts to avoid thoughts, feelings, or conversations associated with the trauma

2. efforts to avoid activities, places, or people that arouse recollections of the trauma

3. inability to recall an important aspect of the trauma

4. markedly diminished interest or participation in significant activities

5. feeling of detachment or estrangement from others

6. restricted range of affect (e.g., unable to have loving feelings)

7. sense of foreshortened future (e.g., does not expect to have a career, marriage, children, or a normal life span)

D. Persistent symptoms of increased arousal (not present before the trauma), as indicated by two (or more) of the following:

1. difficulty falling or staying asleep

2. irritability or outbursts of anger

3. difficulty concentrating

4. hypervigilance

5. exaggerated startle response

E. Duration of the disturbance (symptoms in Criteria B, C, D) is more than 1 month.

F. The disturbance causes clinically significant distress or impairment in social, occupational, or other important areas of functioning.

(*Source:* Reprinted with permission from the *Diagnostic and Statistical Manual of Mental Disorders, Fourth Edition, Text Revision.* Copyright 2000 American Psychiatric Association.)

If the clinical symptoms do not meet these criteria exactly (e.g., the symptoms happen within 1 month of the stressor), the person may be suffering from **acute stress disorder.** The crisis worker should be particularly alert to this possibility. If intervention can be done within the first month, future problems can be prevented, as discussed in Chapter 1.

Diagnostic Criteria for Acute Stress Disorder

The DSM-IV-TR also sets out criteria for acute stress disorder.

A. The person has been exposed to a traumatic event in which both of the following were present:

    1. The person experienced, witnessed, or was confronted with an event or events that involved actual or threatened death or serious injury, or a threat to the physical integrity of self or others.

    2. The person's response involved intense fear, helplessness, or horror.

B. Either while experiencing or after experiencing the distressing event, the individual has three (or more) of the following dissociative symptoms:

    1. a subjective sense of numbing, detachment, or absence of emotional responsiveness

    2. a reduction in awareness of his or her surroundings (e.g., being in a daze)

    3. **derealization**

    4. **depersonalization**

    5. dissociative amnesia (i.e., inability to recall an important aspect of the trauma)

C. The traumatic event is persistently re-experienced in at least one of the following ways: recurrent images, thoughts, dreams, illusions, flashback episodes, or a sense of reliving the experience; or distress on exposure to reminders of the traumatic event.

D. Marked avoidance of stimuli that arouse recollections of the trauma (e.g., thoughts, feelings, conversations, activities, places, people).

E. Marked symptoms of anxiety or increased arousal (e.g., difficulty sleeping, irritability, poor concentration, hypervigilance, exaggerated startle response, motor restlessness).

F. The disturbance causes clinically significant distress or impairment in social, occupational, or other important areas of functioning or impairs the individual's ability to pursue some necessary task, such as obtaining necessary assistance or mobilizing personal resources by telling family members about the traumatic experience.

G. The disturbance lasts for a minimum of 2 days and a maximum of 4 weeks and occurs within 4 weeks of the traumatic event.

H. The disturbance is not due to the direct physiological effects of a substance (e.g., a drug of abuse, a medication) or a general medical condition, is not better accounted for by Brief Psychotic Disorder, and is not merely an exacerbation of a preexisting Axis I or Axis II disorder.

Source: Reprinted with permission from the *Diagnostic and Statistical Manual of Mental Disorders, Fourth Edition, Text Revision.* Copyright 2000 American Psychiatric Association.

There are several different categories of experiences that typically cause PTSD or acute stress disorder. They include being in combat or in a war zone, suffering personal or family victimization, living through a natural disaster, or experiencing a manmade disaster. Each situation creates different emotional experiences for the survivors and different cognitions associated with the trauma. However, survivors of all these experiences tend to have the symptoms of PTSD. A crisis worker is bound to come into contact with clients who did not deal with traumas immediately after they occurred, and so they have most likely been living in some state of PTSD for some time. An event in the present often triggers a memory of the trauma, or the person's functioning may diminish to the point that he or she can't deal with society any longer, so the person seeks the help of a mental health worker.

Some victims exist in a chronic crisis state, never really functioning at all. They often go from one therapist to another or from hospital to jail to clinic looking for coping skills to deal with their current problems. Unfortunately, many cannot be effective in the present until they deal with their past traumas.

Serving in Combat or Living in a War Zone

Counselors first became aware of PTSD when they were dealing with war veterans, especially those of the Vietnam War. Often, they were 19-year-old boys who were sent across the world lacking the coping skills to deal with seeing their buddies blown up and small children killed. Vietnam veterans' symptoms have included re-experiencing the sounds of war, suffering from nightmares, and being unable to manage interpersonal relationships effectively. Support groups were set up to allow these veterans an opportunity to discuss their traumas and find ways to integrate their war experiences into present-day functioning.

The veterans of World War II had similar responses to their combat experiences. Anyone who exhibited signs of trauma was said to have **shell shock**. Unfortunately, World War II veterans did not seek or receive mental health treatment when they returned home. They were encouraged to "buck up" and "be a man." Recent films such as *Saving Private Ryan* have put a realistic perspective on the extent of the trauma experienced by these men. It is easy to forget that they suffered because, unlike their Vietnam veteran counterparts, World War II veterans received a hero's welcome when they returned home. World War II was a popular war, and most Americans were supportive of the efforts of the military.

When soldiers are engaged in combat and see the trauma of war, some do experience acute stress disorder. They are often treated by doctors and given time to recuperate. However, the military does such a good job of training soldiers to numb themselves to war trauma that the majority are able to deal with combat as it is happening. It is when they return home that they show signs of PTSD. The disorder has been delayed, almost by training. Once soldiers return home, many have difficulty adjusting to civilian life. They report being preoccupied with the troops that are still fighting. They often feel guilty for leaving the other soldiers and think they should return to help fight.

The recent wars fought in Iraq and the Persian Gulf have also left emotional scars on combat veterans. Some refer to the PTSD experienced by soldiers who fought to free Kuwait in the 1990s as Persian Gulf syndrome. It is still a bit early to properly identify the effects of combat in the current war against the rebels in Iraq, but since these soldiers are observing killings and other gruesome acts of war, there is little doubt that they will also experience PTSD.

Suffering Personal or Family Victimization

Sadly, we live in a society where people are frequently victimized by others who intend to kill, harm, or intimidate, or all three. The prevalence of child abuse, spousal abuse, and sexual assault is so high that all of Chapter 12 is devoted to these topics. In fact, sexual abuse survivors constitute the largest number of PTSD victims (Shapiro & Forrest, 1997, p. 132).

Many perpetrators of this type of victimization know their victims personally. This adds to the emotional trauma for the victims in ways that "impersonal" traumas such as an earthquake might not. Trust becomes a big issue for people who are attacked by someone they know.

In addition to physical and sexual assault, the following types of trauma may lead to PTSD:

- witnessing a loved one being murdered
- witnessing or being part of a gruesome car accident
- being kidnapped or being the parent of a child who is abducted
- having personal property vandalized (e.g., tires slashed)
- having one's home burglarized
- being robbed at gunpoint

PTSD for survivors of these types of trauma may be severe or mild, depending on the perceived level of threat. They often suffer from feelings of paranoia, **hypervigilance**, and powerlessness. They are usually angry and fearful.

Living Through a Natural Disaster

Natural disasters include landslides, floods, fires, earthquakes, hurricanes, and other storm conditions that wreak havoc on humans. The most recent example was the devastating Hurricane Katrina of 2005, which nearly destroyed the city of New Orleans and caused billions of dollars worth of damage in several states bordering the Gulf of Mexico. As of the writing of this book, the exact death toll is unknown, but this disaster is considered the worst in American history. The flooding of a large area of New Orleans left thousands of people homeless and without food, water, and electricity for several days, until rescue workers arrived to help evacuate those stranded. Several concepts from previous chapters can be observed in the aftermath of this devastating natural disaster.

Material Resources   As was discussed in Chapter 1, individuals with access to material resources such as personal transportation, saving accounts, and home-owner's insurance will undoubtedly manage this crisis more easily than those without them. To start, people who owned cars were able to evacuate New Orleans prior to the hurricane and subsequent flood. Additionally, those who had homeowner's insurance and money in savings accounts will be better able to start over once the acute crisis phase is over and rebuilding begins.

Perception of the Precipitating Event Leads to Subjective Distress   Because of the delay in rescuing many of those stranded in the flood, who had to cling to rooftops for several days, and also the delay in providing food and water for survivors, many survivors and other concerned citizens formed ideas about the reasons for the delays. Many people blamed government officials at all levels for failure to act quickly. This blame led to feelings of rage. When one explores the cognitive tree further, one sees that the blame was fueled by beliefs that racism and classism were reasons for the delays. Because most of the people who needed immediate assistance were poor African Americans, many believed that the failure to rescue and provide was due to the lack of importance given to this subgroup in American culture. This cognition, of course, led to much subjective distress, primarily anger.

Crisis as Danger and Opportunity   As in many other community disasters, people in the United States and around the world responded to Hurricane Katrina with charity and activism. Of course, this disaster has strong elements of danger. People died, homes and businesses were lost, and the historic city of New Orleans was all but destroyed. However, opportunity also arose during this crisis. Americans and people from other countries were enlightened about the disparity that exists between the poor and the upper classes. The disaster provided an opportunity for people to show their humanity, pitch in and help, and engage in dialogue about how to ensure that a similar situation does not occur again.

The catastrophic tsunami that occurred on the coasts of Indochina and other countries in 2004 is another example of the devastation caused by natural disasters. Throughout time, many people have been traumatized by the powerful destruction of earthquakes, blizzards, storms, and floods. These types of disasters make people feel helpless. They may even become angry with God.

When a disaster hits, communities tend to go through certain **phases** to overcome the psychological and physical consequences of the disaster. The Mental Health Center of North Iowa, Inc. (retrieved 6/8/2005) provides information about these phases. The first stage is the heroic phase. This usually occurs during and immediately after the disaster. Emotions are strong and direct. People find themselves being called upon for and responding to demands for heroic action to save their own and others' lives and property. Altruism is prominent, and people expend much energy in helping others to survive and recover. People have a lot of energy and motivation to help. Everyone pitches in to help people that they might not ordinarily have assisted. The second stage is the honeymoon phase, which lasts from 1 week to 6 months after the disaster. There is a strong sense of having shared with others a dangerous, catastrophic experience and having lived through it. Survivors clean out mud and debris from their homes and yards, anticipating that a considerable amount of help will soon be given them to solve their problems. Community groups that are set up to meet specific needs caused by the disaster are important resources during this period. The third stage is the disillusionment phase. When the "honeymoon high" wears off, people realize that life isn't a "bowl of cherries." They realize that people have returned to their normal states of greed, jealousy, and selfishness. The "utopia" they had envisioned doesn't materialize. Strong feelings of disappointment, anger, resentment, and bitterness may arise if promised aid is delayed or never arrives. Outside agencies may leave the affected region, and some community groups may weaken or may not adapt to the changing situation. There is a gradual loss of the feelings of "shared community" as survivors concentrate on rebuilding their lives and solving their own individual problems. The final stage is the reconstruction phase, in which survivors realize that they will need to rebuild their homes, businesses, and lives largely by themselves, and gradually assume the responsibility for doing so. This phase might last for several years following the disaster. Community support groups are essential during this phase as well.

The National Center for Post-Traumatic Stress Disorder (retrieved 6/8/2005) refers to these phases as the impact phase, immediate postdisaster phase, recoil and rescue phase, and recovery phase. The phases are observed when people face natural disasters, personal trauma such as rape (rape trauma syndrome will be discussed in Chapter 12), and manmade disasters.

Surviving a Manmade Disaster

Recall from Chapter 2 that crisis work began when a manmade disaster, the Coconut Grove fire, occurred. Many disasters of this magnitude or worse have occurred since the fire. Sometimes they are accidental, as when a plane crashes; others are perpetrated on purpose and with malicious intent.

World Trade Center and Pentagon Attacks   One such manmade disaster was the terrorist-hijacked airplane crashes into the New York World Trade Center and the U.S. Pentagon on September 11, 2001. These traumas lead to the death of over 5,000 people, the highest disaster-related death toll in U.S. history. Most of us can still remember how the entire country proceeded through the different phases discussed above. The pictures are etched in our minds of men and women working day and night to remove debris from the areas affected by the attacks. This behavior helped to increase feelings of power in all of us. At least something could be done. Unfortunately, this tragedy did not end with the plane crashes but continued with the introduction by terrorists of the anthrax virus into the U.S. Postal System. In 2005, terrorists left bombs in backpacks in the London transit system, reminding us that the threat continues.

A True Story   A powerful story related to the World Trade Center attacks was told to the author by a former student. He had become a sheriff at a local law enforcement agency. After he completed his masters degree in psychology, he was asked to fly to New York and help out. He didn't know exactly what he would be doing, but he was ready to do anything. When he arrived, he went right up to the emergency workers, firefighters, and police, who were heaving heavy cement pieces from Ground Zero, searching for bodies. They were sweating, breathing heavily, and crying. He started helping them, until one of the workers told him to stop. The student said, "But I'm here to help." The worker looked at him and with tears in his eyes said, "This is our job. Your job is to take care of us. There are over 600 people in that building over there who need someone to talk to, share their feelings with, and we hope you can do this." The student walked over to the building and was met by hundreds of people that had been working day and night, survivors of the attacks, and people who had lost loved ones in the attacks. At this point, he certainly felt needed. He was able to use the ABC model that he had just learned to help these people begin to put their lives back together.

Oklahoma City Federal Building Bombing   The bombing of the Oklahoma City federal building in April 1995 is yet another example of a monumental disaster, in which more than 200 people, including preschool children, were killed and many others injured. Complete crisis intervention and critical incident debriefing services were needed to help the survivors of this bombing and of the New York City attack, as well as people in the community, deal with these traumas.

INTERVENTIONS

When disasters happen, they affect not only those directly involved but others who suddenly feel that their security is threatened. Communities throughout the United States responded to the recent traumatic events by providing much-needed support.

Examples of community support included relief funds for families of the victims, generous donations to the **Red Cross,** and crisis response units established in a variety of locales such as elementary schools and even public parks. The crisis intervention was aimed at helping children and adults deal with beliefs that the community is no longer a safe place. Shock that something like this could happen to "me and my family" was a common response by many. Crisis workers needed to help people think differently about the situation, showing the secondary victims through education and empowerment statements that they could cope with this situation.

To function during an emergency situation, people must put their feelings and normal human reactions aside. This state of denial allows individuals to act in order to survive. If this initial shock did not exist, people would be so overwhelmed with feelings that they could not function at all. After the emergency is stabilized, those involved can come to terms at an appropriate pace with what has happened. This process is referred to as a delayed reaction and is the basis for PTSD.

The tendency is for individuals who have been traumatized to seek resolution at some point in some way. This resolution takes a variety of forms and may occur at conscious as well as unconscious levels. For example, nightmares that replay the event are common in PTSD. It is as if the unconscious mind is trying to help the person bring closure to the trauma by creating stress at night so the person will be motivated to deal with the trauma in a wakeful, conscious state.

Once individuals have allowed the trauma to surface, floods of feelings are aroused. Professional help is then needed to channel those feelings into productive avenues for growth. As with all crisis situations, people need to see that some new meaning can be ascribed to even the most devastating trauma. Victor Frankl's work on logotherapy (meaning therapy) is a good example; it shows how he used his trauma as a Nazi concentration camp survivor to create growth in himself as a person. Despite the catastrophic nature of his experience, he found a way to see meaning in it. This ability no doubt helped him survive psychologically.

If people do not receive help after a trauma, the posttraumatic symptoms get worse over time, and the individuals learn to adjust to life in a less functional way. Such people will have less psychic energy available for dealing with daily stresses, because they are using their energy to continue to deny the feelings associated with the trauma. These people will most likely have difficulty in interpersonal relationships, which require feelings if they are to be at all satisfying.

Critical Incident and Debriefing

Because of the extent of manmade and natural disasters, mental health professionals have developed special programs and training that focus on helping people and communities overcome the effects of traumas, or critical incidents. All of the traumas discussed so far in this chapter are examples of critical incidents. Some mental health professionals refer to this process as trauma response or **disaster mental health** (Ladrech, 2004). Special training programs are available for workers wanting to help victims of disasters through the Red Cross and other responding organizations such as the International Medical Corps. Disaster mental health is a crisis intervention method that "stabilizes, supports and normalizes people in an effort to strengthen their coping abilities, and hopefully, prevent long-term damage such as PTSD, substance abuse, depression, and family and relationship problems. It is not meant to be treatment" (Ladrech, 2004, p. 21).

There are a few special considerations to keep in mind when dealing with people who have experienced a critical incident. The Los Angeles County Department of Mental Health (2001) has listed common signs and signals of a stress reaction to a traumatic event. Most of these symptoms correspond to those listed in the above definition of PTSD. This information is useful for crisis workers so that they may educate victims of trauma about the normalcy of such symptoms. Knowing that these symptoms are typical may relieve victims who thought they were going "crazy."

Physical signs include fatigue, nausea, muscle tremors, twitches, chest pain, difficulty breathing, elevated blood pressure, rapid heart rate, thirst, visual difficulties, vomiting, grinding of teeth, weakness, dizziness, profuse sweating, chills, shock symptoms, and fainting. Typical emotional and behavioral signs of critical incident stress include anxiety, guilt, grief, panic, fear, uncertainty, loss of emotional control, depression, irritability, apprehension, change in activity, change in speech patterns, withdrawal, outbursts, suspiciousness, loss or increase of appetite, alcohol consumption, antisocial acts, pacing, hyper-alertness, and startle reflex.

There may also be cognitive symptoms such as blaming, confusion, poor attention, poor decisions, poor concentration, memory problems, increased or decreased awareness of surroundings, poor abstract thinking, loss of time, place, or person, nightmares, and intrusive images. Counselors should assess whether these symptoms are due to a serious mental disorder such as schizo-phrenia or part of the PTSD.

Red Cross workers (2001) suggest that these initial symptoms may change over time and have observed certain responses occurring in the weeks and months following a critical incident. Sometimes, a person may not connect these symptoms to the trauma because of the time that has elapsed between the symptoms and the incident. Crying for no apparent reason; apathy and depression; frustration and feelings of powerlessness; increased effects of aller-gies, colds, and flu; moodiness; disappointment with, and rejection of, outside help; isolation; guilt about not being able to prevent the disaster; and domes-tic violence are common delayed responses. Table 11.1 provides a summary of the causes and symptoms of PTSD.

Effects on Young Children

Children may be prone to exhibit certain behaviors after exposure to a trauma. These symptoms are similar to those seen in abused children. The following behaviors are common in young children after a critical incident:

- returning to earlier behavior, such as thumb sucking or bed wetting
- clinging to parents
- being reluctant to go to bed
- having nightmares
- having fantasies that the disaster never happened
- crying and screaming
- withdrawing and becoming immobile
- refusing to attend school
- having problems at school and being unable to concentrate (American Red Cross, 2001)

Debriefing Process

The **debriefing process** after a critical incident follows the same process as the ABC model of crisis intervention and uses Caplan's model regarding charac-teristics of people coping effectively (see Chapter 1). According to both the American Red Cross (2001) and the Los Angeles County Department of Mental Health (2001), coping with stressful situations begins with listening

TABLE 11.1 | **SUMMARY OF PTSD CAUSES AND SYMPTOMS**

Posttraumatic stress disorder (PTSD)

Causes	Real or perceived threat or harm to oneself or close loved ones
Symptoms	Recurring nightmares, re-experiencing the event, hypervigilance, anxiety, sleeplessness, numbness, dissociation
Precipitating events	Loved one is murdered or dies in accident suddenly; assault; rape; war; bombings

Types of PTSD

Acute stress disorder	Symptoms of PTSD lasting only 1 month
Delayed PTSD	When situation is not dealt with, person uses defenses to cope, so symptoms subside until something triggers an acute reaction

and empathizing. Both groups further suggest that traumatized persons need someone to spend time with them. Support and reassurance about safety is critical, as is respecting the need to grieve losses. Support statements that tell the person you're sorry the event occurred are better than statements such as, "You're lucky it wasn't worse." It is also helpful to encourage the traumatized person to talk to others about the trauma and accept help from others. Providing information about special assistance for victims of the traumatic event is vital. Crisis interventionists should also help people to be tolerant of irritability in others and redefine priorities and focus energy on those priorities. This is similar to Caplan's suggestions about pacing oneself and breaking tasks down into manageable bits.

Traumatized people should be encouraged to function where possible and maintain healthy eating habits and sleep patterns. Actively seeking information about the trauma should be encouraged as well.

The crisis worker should be well informed about community support groups. Talking with others who have experienced the same trauma is helpful. Any educational statements, empowerment statements, support statements, or reframes are useful and helpful with the person and the family.

Other Therapeutic Approaches Commonly Used to Treat PTSD

According to the National Center for Post-Traumatic Stress Disorder (2005), the first phase of treatment with PTSD survivors and their families includes educating them about how people get PTSD and how it affects survivors and their loved ones, and other problems that are commonly associated with PTSD symptoms. It is helpful to inform people that PTSD is a medically recognized anxiety disorder that occurs in normal individuals under extremely stressful conditions. Another aspect of this first phase of treatment is exposure to the event via imagery, as this allows survivors to re-experience the event in a safe, controlled environment as they examine their reactions and beliefs about it. It is also necessary to have clients examine and resolve strong feelings such as anger, shame, or guilt, which are common in survivors of trauma.

Cognitive-behavioral techniques such as teaching clients how to engage in deep breathing and relaxation exercises, manage anger, prepare for future stress reactions, handle future trauma, and communicate and relate effectively with people are useful.

A relatively new treatment approach for traumatic memories, **eye movement desensitization and reprocessing (EMDR)**, involves elements of exposure therapy and cognitive-behavioral therapy. The theory and research are still evolving for this form of treatment, but there is some evidence that it may facilitate the accessing and processing of traumatic material (Shapiro, 2002). For clients who do not respond to brief crisis intervention, trained EMDR therapists are an invaluable resource in overcoming PTSD.

Group therapy is also a good resource. Trauma survivors can share traumatic material within an atmosphere of safety, cohesion, and empathy provided by other survivors. By sharing their feelings of shame, fear, anger, and self-condemnation, survivors are enabled to resolve many issues related to their trauma.

Medication may be necessary for some trauma survivors. It can reduce the anxiety, depression, and insomnia often experienced. It is useful for relieving symptoms so that the survivor is able to participate in psychological treatment.

Case Vignettes

Practice the ABC model with the following cases. Try to incorporate the information from this chapter about critical incident debriefing and community response and trauma response models.

Case 1   An 11-year-old boy saw his grandfather killed in a car accident while they were vacationing in Mexico. He cannot concentrate in school and refuses to go anywhere in a car.

Hint: Assess for other PTSD symptoms.

Hint: Give support and validation statements about how traumatic this experience was.

Hint: Assess cognitions about the accident. Does he feel guilty for surviving?

Hint: Reframe that his grandfather wouldn't want him to do poorly in school because of this event.

Hint: Let him talk.

Hint: Educate about car accidents and how to be safe.

Case 2   A 40-year-old college professor went to the parking lot after work and found that three tires on her car were flat. They had been slashed by a knife. She is paranoid, thinks someone is out to get her, and constantly worries about her car being vandalized again. She is hypervigilant and notices every minute change in her environment. She is not able to have fun any more.

Hint: Educate about PTSD.

Hint: Give support statements about how scary this situation would be.

Hint: Empower by pointing out that by not enjoying life, she lets the **perpetrator** continue to victimize her.

Hint: Reframe the paranoia as having been appropriate for a brief time, but now her fears are working against her, not for her.

Case 3 A 33-year-old city worker was squatting on one knee, fixing a fire hydrant, when a man held a knife to his throat and told him to hand over his wallet. Since then, he has not been able to work, cannot sleep, and will not let his children go out at night.

Hint: Support his fears.

Hint: Let him talk.

Hint: Educate about PTSD.

Hint: Empower him.

Case 4 An 8-year-old boy was brought in by his parents after a magnitude 6.6 earthquake occurred in his town. He is anxious all the time and won't play. He perseverates about the earthquake and says he has nightmares all the time.

Hint: Educate the parents and the child about PTSD.

Hint: Let the child talk.

Hint: Educate about earthquakes.

KEY TERMS FOR STUDY

acute stress disorder: A condition that occurs within 1 month of a severe trauma. The symptoms are the same as for PTSD.

critical incident: A serious trauma that often causes PTSD.

debriefing: Intervention after a person has been assessed to be affected by a critical incident. It includes listening, empathizing, educating, and supporting.

depersonalization: PTSD sufferer no longer feels like his or her normal self. Person has trouble connecting personally with others.

derealization: People suffering from PTSD often feel that life is not the same and things don't seem real. They feel as though they are walking around in a fog.

disaster mental health: A specialty field of mental health treatment in which counselors are trained how to respond with people after they have experienced some form of community disaster. Often referred to as *trauma response*.

dissociation: A defense mechanism that assists people who have experienced trauma to continue to function. They split off from the terror and fear of the event and push their feelings into their subconscious.

EMDR (eye movement desensitization and reprocessing): A type of treatment for PTSD that combines cognitive, behavioral, and exposure therapies.

hypervigilance: A state of preparedness and anxiety that often occurs after someone has been personally attacked.

perpetrators: Individuals who purposefully victimize and intimidate others, usually for purposes of gaining power and relieving feelings of frustration and anger.

phases of community disaster: Conceptualization that communities experience certain stages during and after a serious disaster: heroic phase, honeymoon phase, disillusionment phase, and reconstruction phase.

PTSD (posttraumatic stress disorder): Condition that occurs when people have been severely traumatized and are not functioning effectively. They demonstrate a variety of anxiety and depressive symptoms.

Red Cross: An international organization established to assist people worldwide when disaster strikes.

shell shock: A term used for the veterans of World War II who showed symptoms of PTSD.